When you pray
    God listens to you
When you meditate
    God talks to you
Listen and you will
here
    God messages to you

        Theresa
        Orecchio

Whispering
Messages

T M Orecchia

BALBOA.
PRESS
A DIVISION OF HAY HOUSE

Balboa Press books may be ordered through booksellers or by contacting:

Balboa Press
A Division of Hay House
1663 Liberty Drive
Bloomington, IN 47403
www.balboapress.com
1 (877) 407-4847

Print information available on the last page.

ISBN: 978-1-5043-6741-7 (sc)
ISBN: 978-1-5043-6743-1 (hc)
ISBN: 978-1-5043-6742-4 (e)

Library of Congress Control Number: 2016916542

Balboa Press rev. date: 10/06/2016

CONTENTS

DEDICATION

To my very kind and loving husband, Michael V. Orecchia, whose dedication and deeply caring heart has given me a wonderful journey in our thirty three years of marriage. Michael has taught me to stand tall and believe in myself no matter the chatter behind my back. His strength has powered me through many difficult times...the loss of my first husband, Edwin G Northup, in the Vietnam war, the loss of both of my parents who were always a special part of my life, and for his urging and supporting me to return to school at the age of forty five for my pharmacy degree!

Michael is my number one book fan! He happily supported the publishing of my previous two books, *Hear Their Voices* and *Receive Their Messages*. He has also served as my 'editor-in-chief' for all of my projects. He has tirelessly given his time and love to me since we have been together. I could not have accomplished all that I have without his support, time and love. With that, I say 'thank you' God for sending me one of your 'finest'. You have made my life complete with Michael.

Michael, thank you for all that you have given me especially your love. I cherish it dearly and hold you very close to my heart.

ACKNOWLEDGEMENTS

Working with Jesus has been a delightful experience. The messages that were channeled to me started off as evening conversations with Jesus during meditations. We sometimes bantered back and forth and that was fun. Many times I interjected with a 'but' or 'that doesn't make sense' and He always stopped to explain exactly what He was saying and how I could apply it to my life. I recorded these meditative thoughts for about a year. As I was reviewing my recordings recently, I realized there were many profound messages in His words that could benefit the world.

Thank you Jesus for giving me your 'words of wisdom'. Thank you also for your expert editing advice for each message that was used.

A special thank you goes to my nephew, Ron F. Sill, for his talented and unique artwork. It is always a pleasure working with Ron. I can give him a thought and even before I finish, he is sketching several ideas that we expand on. Thank you, Ron.

I would also like to thank the angels and archangels who surround me when I channel. It is always comforting to know and feel their presence as they guard me.

I would like to especially thank my wonderful husband, Michael, for all the time he committed to me for this project. He tirelessly helped me edit the manuscript from the original conversations that I had recorded to the final copy. I am sure he can recite a couple of the messages from memory. Thank you, Michael, from the bottom of my heart.

INTRODUCTION

I AM ALL THAT I AM

You have heard that expression before. It is all encompassing. It represents the power of the universe. It is the power of all. It is the beginning and the end. In short, it is the Source of the Universe.

The following meditative compositions were channeled from a higher source to help those on earth evaluate their everyday lives and realign their hearts to God. By realigning with God while on earth, humans can change their lives and return to the development of their souls.

Read each passage carefully then think about it. Think about your life and how each passage applies to your current life style.

Are you aligned with what the message is saying?

Do you need to change your lifestyle to open your mind and soul to move closer to God?

Do you need to rediscover your soul?

Is it important to you?

Have you chosen to put your soul development on the back burner at this time in your life or should you seriously evaluate the status of your soul?

Whispering Messages is just that --- 'whispering' words of advice.

Receive them with love and open your heart to receive the words of the higher realms of God.

WIND

*B*e quiet.

Be still.

Listen to the wind. It is talking to you. It is singing to you.

Don't be afraid.

Does it sound joyful to you? Does it sound sorrowful to you?

Look into your heart. Listen to your heart for it will tell you what the wind is saying.

Only you will know the answer.

The wind is talking to you as God is talking to you. Sometimes it is strong and forceful, sometimes it is soft and gentle…and sometimes it is even smiling.

Your heart knows because that is where God resides in you.

A hardened heart is like a locked door to God. He does not have the key to open it.

As you are quiet, contemplating and listening, can you hear God? Can you hear His whispers of love to you?

They are there but only you can hear them and only you can let His messages of love into your heart.

Sit for a while and focus on the wind then focus on your heart, can you hear Him? Stay with Him, and enjoy this time with God. He loves to visit you.

When you are finished, open your eyes and each time you hear the wind whispering, smile and be happy for God is truly in your heart.

-Jesus

OCEAN

What is more refreshing than going to the ocean and hearing the sound of the surf and feeling the wind blowing through your hair.

Have you ever thought about it? Have you ever thought how cleansing it is to your soul and how peaceful you feel?

Stay there and enjoy this peace. Let it penetrate every cell in your body.

For in the wind and the ocean spray that blows onto your face there I am…I am peace, I am love. Receive me. Let me into your heart so you may feel my love for you.

My love surrounds you constantly when you open your heart to me. Don't be afraid of this peaceful feeling because it is yours to enjoy. Receive it deeply. Put it in a special place in your heart.

When you return to the hustle of living and stress is on your doorstep, stop and remember your day at the ocean. Go to that special place in your heart and be quiet. Bring forth the inner peace that you placed into your heart. Move it throughout your body. Let it penetrate. Now give me your stress. Breathe deeply. Doesn't that feel good? Your head feels lighter and your body feels lighter. Happiness surrounds you.

Now go on with your day and be happy for I am with you always.

Remember me.

Remember the peace in your heart.

-Jesus

DANCING LEAVES

*W*alking quietly as the evening approaches, the wind stirs the leaves around your feet.

You look down and smile with a childhood memory of leaves falling in rhythm with the wind.

The wind is gently talking to you again. Listen as you did when you were a child.

The leaves are dancing happily around you.

It is very quiet but you suddenly feel surrounded by love.

Look around and you will see no one. Now look inside your mind, inside your heart and you will see me. You will see my angels.

We are walking with you and talking with you. Can you hear us? Can you hear our whispers in the wind?

Be very still, walk slowly and listen…listen to your heart.

What are you hearing? What are you feeling? Are you feeling love growing stronger around you? Are you getting pictures in your mind of happiness and love? What do they look like? What do they feel like? Are words of love and peace coming to you?

My angels and I are sending these feelings and words to you for we are with the wind and the dancing leaves. Receive us into your heart and receive our love.

Don't discard these feelings when you arrive home. Keep them in your heart. When you are sad or when you feel alone, remember the wind. Remember the dancing leaves and remember our love... it is in your heart.

We are always walking with you. Hear us, feel us and see us.

We are the dancing leaves in the wind. We are the wind.

-Jesus

CLOUDS

*S*oft, white clouds move gently across the sky. They bring beauty to all who take a moment to stop and reflect on God's artistic hand.

Many of you will notice this beauty but as the clouds join together and darken with a chilly wind, fear may rise in your heart. What once was a friendly, loving and soft white cloud is now viewed as an ominous threat.

But look at these clouds, as you would look at God.

You may like to identify God as a white, fluffy and lovable cloud that is easy to love, easy to understand, easy to believe in and easy to follow.

But many times the white, fluffy clouds darken and these dark clouds may scare you. They are big and strong and capable of bringing about change. Can you see God in these large and powerful dark clouds? Do you look the other way or flee because you are afraid of God when you see His power?

God loves you and is always ready to help you but God is also demanding when it comes to walking His path.

So, think about your life now…what path are you following? Do you want to change? Do you want to be closer to God?

It will not be easy, but remember the dark storm clouds and their power. That is God. Stand tall with the storm clouds, and stand tall with God, and don't be afraid to change.

Call on me. I know God and I know you. I am here for you. With my help, you can change your present path in life.

We will both see God smiling on you as the dark storm clouds of your life change back to soft, white clouds surrounded by angels.

-Jesus

RAIN

*D*o you like a rainy day? It can be music to your ears with the steady beat of the raindrops on the windshield of your car or on the windows of your home.

Did you ever meditate with the rain and the soothing rhythm of the raindrops?

Did you ever feel the calm and the quiet that surrounds a rainy day?

The peace you feel when you stop to enjoy the rain is truly the peace of God.

He is always there to give you the peace and love that you are looking for. You don't have to search far…just look to the rain. Look to the rhythm of the rain.

Listen to the rain for He is talking to you. Can you hear Him? What is your heart saying? Do you need to go deeper into your heart or do you need to back up and clear the noise from your head? Take your time for He is patient. God will always wait for you.

If you want to take small steps, that is okay too. Go at your own pace. If anything, just enjoy the sound of the rain and the peace that enters your heart. The more you come to this place of peace with the rain, the easier it is to quiet your mind and open your heart to God.

Don't worry…He will be there for you no matter how long it takes. As you get more comfortable in turning inward to your heart and to God, your life will open fully to you.

You will truly see the beauty of God wherever you go and with whomever you meet.

You will always feel His love in your heart.

Enjoy the rainy day and receive God to the fullest.

-Jesus

MOUNTAINS

*Y*ou ask me many times where am I and I tell you that I am everywhere.

That is true, you say, but you still don't see me. So I ask you, why not?

You say that you have tried very hard to see me but nothing happens. And I say that is because you are looking the wrong way.

Go and look at the beautiful, majestic mountains. You say…they are beautiful but where is God in all this because I am looking at mountains and not God. Look again and look real hard. Now, what do you see? Mountains, you answer. Look again; look deeply into the mountains. Do you see God? You say that you believe that you are starting to see God.

Now that you are beginning to see God in the majestic beauty of the mountains, look into your heart. What do you feel? Do you feel happy? Do you feel love?

Let's start with happy. As you look very deeply into the mountain landscape, happiness is your first feeling. You are very happy to have this opportunity to experience the majesty of the mountains. You are very happy that you took the time out of your busy schedule to enjoy the beauty of nature and be with God.

Now, you are ready to experience love… the love that emanates from this majestic mountain scene. The love you now feel is God. He is in the mountains. He is in the valleys and streams and trees. It is God who composes the entire scene.

Close your eyes and breathe deeply. Feel God's presence. Stay there for a few minutes. Know that you are experiencing the love that God has for you.

You are now enjoying newfound feelings of peace and love. Realize you feel very comfortable in this place of love. You feel that you truly belong there.

Now, you are not necessarily falling in love with the mountains per se. You are falling back in love with God. You have been reunited with God. You are back home with Him and that is why you are so comfortable.

Return to this mountain scene in your mind as often as you can. Go home to God. He loves your company.

-Jesus

HEAR THE NOISE

*T*he streets are crowded. The streets are noisy. You hustle and weave your way through a massive number of people, most of them coming at you. You look at your watch, checking the time to see if you must quicken your pace to make your appointment. Your heart is pounding, your adrenaline is flowing, and your feet just can't seem to move fast enough.

But I say to you now, take a deep breath, slow down, listen to the music and arrive at your meeting with a smile on your face. What music, you say. There is just street traffic, noise and lots of people in a hurry.

Listen again.

There is a rhythm to the horns blowing, a rhythm to the moving traffic, and a rhythm to the busy people. Listen carefully and hear that rhythm. With each step you take, there is a beat. Walk with that beat. Feel the beat. Enjoy the beat. Go with the blowing horns, go with the sounds of the buses and go with the blinking streetlights at each corner. Go deep inside yourself to make this rhythm a part of you.

As you do this, be aware of your feet. They are starting to pick up the rhythm you are feeling. Go with that movement. Feel that movement. Now you are in-tune with all that is around you. With all the perceived chaos in your life today, you have just taken the time to let the angels into your life.

Look at the people walking towards you. They see you and they smile at you. A few even say hello. They see your peace. They see your inner glow and your oneness with God. The world may appear very chaotic to you but it is only your eyes that make it so.

When you see this chaos, and your life becomes frenzied, remember to stop. Stop for just one minute. Look around you. Look for the angels and look for the rhythm. It is there but YOU must open your eyes and heart to find it. Try it. You will be surprised by all the 'smiles' and 'hellos' that come your way.

When you become completely engulfed with God's love, chaos will become a stranger in your life.

-Jesus

OPEN YOUR HEART

I come many times to the earth realm but no one really sees or hears me.

I have come many times to you but you only see the distractions in your life. You see the glitter, and the tinsel. You say you didn't see me because life's distractions WERE stronger. You say that I need to shine MY light brighter. But I say to you, you are not looking for me.

I hear your words many times in petitions but I don't see any actions. I come to answer your requests but you walk away from me. You do not see me; you do not hear or listen to me. I want to be a part of your life but you must let me into your heart.

When life becomes difficult for you and you believe there is no possible human answer, you always come to me for help. But know that I am here to help you not only in difficult times but also at all times. When you open your heart to me, you will hear me, and you will see me.

I hear you asking me now…how can I 'hear' you? How can I 'see' you? I tell you that it is easy but you must remove the noise from your mind. Once you trust me and open your mind and heart to me, you will stop worrying about the difficulties in your life. You will exude an air of confidence, an air of love and compassion. Many will be drawn to you like a magnet.

When you open your heart, you will see these changes occurring and you will know they are coming from me. Your life will begin to change. It will be gradual at first but you will recognize the changes. Your confidence will grow and you will call on me more frequently because you will like your new life.

I sense your doubts moving in. You wonder…how long will this last? Is this for real? Am I just being overzealous with my meditative thoughts? Trust me, this is for real. Only you can bring an end to your successful and happy life by doubting yourself, and by doubting your belief in my power. No one can bring you down except you and no one can raise you up except you.

Open your heart and let me help you.

-Jesus

ALL ARE ONE

$\mathcal{W}$hy do you humans think you are superior to one another?

You look at each other and evaluate your features, your color, and your mannerisms and you look for common links between you. And those common links then ensure that it is okay to associate with each other.

Why is it important to have a common link? Why do you think you are more privileged because you live in a highly civilized country compared to those who live in a less developed country? Why do you feel superior because you are college educated? Why do you feel you are 'above' the manual laborer or farm worker because you have an office job, or a big city job?

Well, let me tell you, every human on earth is equal to each other. There are no favorites. There are no special personalities no matter their station in life. All are from God, and He loves them equally. Why don't you?

Who are you to judge all the different character traits created by God? He loves them all. No matter how you judge another human, remember, in God's eyes all humans are His children and He loves everyone.

So you say to yourself, if we are all God's children why are we all so different? Why are we on different levels on the ladder to success? So I say to you, what is the ladder of success? You equate success with financial rewards. Have you looked inside lately, inside your soul, that is? What is the success of your soul? What good is financial success without soul success? And who are you to judge how others live their lives? That is not of your concern. Your main concern in your lifetime on earth is to develop your own soul and move closer to God.

Remember the street vendor on the corner at lunchtime selling hot sandwiches and fruit? Remember the children going to school in a poor neighborhood with sweaters on their backs instead of coats to protect them from the cold? Remember the pictures of people walking to another country to escape oppression? Why do you think you are better than these people? They are all with God and each is intent on developing their soul in the environment presented to them at birth.

Open your heart as you evaluate the people around you and know they may be more advanced than you in their soul development process.

There is no time for prejudice. There is no time for hatred.

Know that God loves you exactly as He loves those whom you don't love.

-Jesus

REMEMBER LOVE

*R*emember when you were small and surrounded by total love from your parents, from your aunts and uncles, and even your cousins and friends? That feeling of love was wonderful. You were so happy when all these people bestowed their love on you. It seemed never-ending.

Ah, but then, you grew up. Where did the love go?

This love continues to surround you but you do not feel it as strongly as when you were young. As you grow older you recognize it less and less. Sometimes you even reject it.

Do you think this love was just from your family and friends? No, this love was from me. I shower you with love every day starting from the day you were born. When you reject your parents or even your friends at different times in your life, you reject me. They love you as I love you. I work through many to shower you with love.

Look at your interactions with your friends and your family. When you evoke sad feelings in another, you are sending them sadness with your statements. Wake up and be aware. Those around you love you. They want an interaction with you that is telling them you are receiving their love.

As your parents and relatives age, remember the love they gave you as a child. Return this love to them; they need it, for they are frightened. They know their life on earth will end in a short time and they know and believe in an afterlife but this is the time when reality hits home. They taught you for many years to believe in God and His angels but now they are approaching heaven's threshold and they are frightened of the unknown. Give them your love, and give them my love. Look at their souls not their humanity. This may difficult for you but grow your soul, step over your inhibitions and extend your hand to them as you give them your love.

Always remember the love bestowed upon you as a child and return that love to as many people as you can as an adult. Remember your love is my love.

Think about it.

Who would refuse my love?

And if my love is your love, who would refuse your love and thus refuse me?

-Jesus

REMEMBER ME

*T*he young baby laughs and giggles for no reason. Isn't that cute, you say, without wondering any further why the child is suddenly so happy. The child is playing with the angels. Angels are always with the children. They are even with you as an adult but you have forgotten.

Children see the angels and remember their spiritual life with me and with the angels. It makes them happy to see us again. They know they are not alone on earth.

But as you age, you do not remember or see us any more. Yes, it is easy to forget me. But I understand. Life on earth is very fast and demanding and humans are thrown many curve balls to distract them. But if you would remember me, and call on me, you could handle all of life's curve balls without 'batting an eye' as the saying goes.

Remember your best friend who just came down with cancer and the flurry of activity with their family as all your friends came together to decide how to help and support your friend at this difficult time? But no one called on me!

I was there. I was waiting for you but many of your prayers just asked for help for your friend. You needed help too. The angels and archangels were already surrounding and preparing your friend to walk through this challenging time but what about you and your friends? Did you ever get together to talk about how this event was affecting you?

I am here always for you no matter how big or small your problem may be. But you don't need a problem to contact me. Come and talk to me as you would talk with your mother, your father, your spouse, or your best friend. I won't holler at you. I won't criticize you. I just want to listen to you.

As you develop this skill of talking to me, you will begin to hear my messages. You may hear the same message several times and that is because I am trying to get your attention to listen and focus on what I am saying. It is important that you understand it completely so you can make it a part of your life.

Remember me daily. Remember me when you are alone or lonely. Remember me when you are frightened. Remember me when you are happy or frustrated or desperate. Remember the happy times of your childhood with me.

Remember me.

-Jesus

I AM WITH YOU

*Y*ou hear. You see. You feel. You know that I am with you but many times you forget.

You fear. You panic. You feel alone and again you forget that I am with you.

I have always been with you from the day you were born. You talked to me many times when you were a child but you grew up and grew away from me.

You are here, reading this note. Know that I brought you here to awaken you to me, to make you aware that I am with you even when you don't feel or hear me.

Remember how you always asked me, when you were a child, to protect you against the dark because you were afraid? You knew then that I was with you and that I would protect you. Give me your fears again. It is not just for children to give me their fears. I want to hear from the children who are adults now. I want to know YOUR fears, YOUR anxieties, and YOUR doubts.

Life on earth is not easy and no one said it was. Fear, anxiety, and doubt are non-existent when you are aware that I am with you.

How do you return to me, you ask?

It is very easy. Just say 'hello' to me every morning when you open your eyes. Say hello and welcome me into your day. I know you and I know your fears, your anxieties, and your doubts. As your fears, anxieties and doubts rise during the day, I will quiet them for you.

Continue this practice of calling on me every morning. You will become calmer and more in-tune with your inner-self. Life will go on as usual for you until one day, someone or something pushes all of your buttons but you will handle each occurrence with ease. It is then, and only then, that you will realize that something is changing in your life.

You have now opened your heart and you clearly see that I am with you.

I am always with you.

-Jesus

AWAKEN TO ME

*N*ow that you are starting to awaken to me, stand tall and be proud when people say that you look different; you look alive and happy.

It is I. I am becoming a part of your life. You have allowed me to come into your life and into your heart. Realize how happy you are and how peaceful your heart is.

I know you will drift back to your past lifestyle, but I enjoy being with you again. I enjoy making you happy and peaceful.

It is easy to return to me for I am always with you. Make the effort to concentrate on me. Make time for me each day. Meditate on my name. This process is slow because it is always hard to change your lifestyle. Remember, I am not asking you to change your life completely. I am just asking you to make me a part of it.

When you empty your mind, think only of me. When you look at the clouds, the trees, and the birds, think only of me. I am there with you. You must look for me. When you look for me, you will then begin to hear me and hear my messages.

I am with you. I have been with you from the day you were born and I will remain with you until the day you return to me.

When you see me, you will hear me. When you hear me, you will know me.

I am your lifeline. Use me.

I know you as God knows you and as you know yourself.

Come and awaken to me.

-Jesus

WALK WITH ME

I watch you every day as you struggle through life and I am very proud of you. Now come walk with me and I will show you a peaceful path in life.

Always remember that no one is born unhappy. Everyone is born with a life plan or goal to accomplish on earth. It is a challenge. The soul is very happy to have this challenge and the opportunity to come to earth and live their written life plan.

Many times, irritable humans cross your path and I see you sometimes get impatient. You don't want to be bothered. However, if you look closely, you will see that their souls are very sad. They are sad because they are moving away from their written plan on earth. They are not recognizing their soul and thus turning to you for help.

Why me, you say. It is you because I know that you are close to me and I can work through you. This is a challenging task. When you are confronted with an irritable person don't become impatient. Turn to me for guidance. My angels and I are your support system. Call on us and we will show you how to guide and support the soul that is leaning on your shoulder. Remember, I am working through you.

So, as you continue through life, remember me. Come and walk with me for this is life and I am very much a part of it. I am with you and I am with those who come to you for help.

Life is not easy, but with your inner buddy system, that is the angels and I, life is really worth living. It is worth traveling through.

Remember, when all else fails and you are at your wits end, call my name and know that I am walking beside you.

-Jesus

LISTEN

*S*hush. Be very quiet.

Can you hear me? Are you listening?

Life is very busy for you and I really DO understand why you have difficulty hearing me.

I talk to you every day but you say that you don't have time to be quiet right now to listen to me. But I say to you, when is the right time? Don't try to justify your busy life. If you do, you will never have time to listen to me.

Many times, you walk down a grocery aisle, and stop and stare at the shelves. You forget what you are looking for...that is because I am trying to talk to you. When this happens, turn down an aisle in the grocery store where you know that you don't need anything and walk slowly. Now, give me one minute of your time. Whisper my name. Wait a second and then feel my love enter your soul. You suddenly feel this overwhelming peace in your heart. You smile without knowing why and other shoppers return your smile and say hello as they pass. In that short minute, you have let me into your heart. You listened and heard my voice.

You have many thoughts moving through your mind each day. Try to quiet those thoughts when you can because a quiet mind hears my words easily. Each time you have a short, quiet moment, think of me. Think of me and then just listen. Listen for my words of support, my words of love, my words of laughter and my words of wellbeing. I am always with you so all you have to do is just listen.

It is easy.

Try it. Try it today. Try it now. You will be surprised how love truly feels in your heart.

It is my love that is entering your heart and it is waiting for you to receive it.

Shush now. Be quiet. Listen and receive my love.

-Jesus

WHERE ARE YOU

*W*here are you?

I have been looking for you. I have been waiting for you to call me. I miss you.

Oh, I know you are busy. Everyone on earth is busy.

You were with me as a child and sometimes as a young adult. But as you progressed in life and in your career, you drifted away from me. I understand. But why don't you just call me? I see you call and text your family and friends every day. Am I not a part of your family? You always said goodnight to me as a child when you knelt at your bedside and said your prayers to your guardian angels and to me. I miss that. I miss you.

Where are you? Why are you walking through life without my help and without the help of my angels? Life can be very difficult. My angels and I can help you because we can show you how to navigate the many paths of life.

Why should I call you, you ask. 'Can you give me the money for my rent? Can you give me money for my child's medical bills? Can you give me money to just buy groceries? No, I cannot give you money for all this, but I CAN show you 'the way' to accomplish your goals. I will 'advise' you. Trust me when I say that I can give you advice.

Nothing is too complicated for us to help you and keep you on your life's plan. But it is up to you to communicate with me and communicate with my angels. Let us into your heart. Talk to us daily. You talk and even complain to your family and friends but what can THEY do? Talk to me and I will direct you to the assistance you need.

But you must LISTEN when you ask me for help and guidance. I will send you messages. You will hear them as thoughts and as ideas. Pay attention and follow those ideas. The more you talk to me, the more skilled you will become at following my messages. Now, one day you may think you just got a crazy idea about how to change a difficult situation in your life…don't dismiss that thought. Think about it because it is I sending you help. Angels are also surrounding you, giving you signs and messages to follow. Don't ignore them. When difficult times come your way…remember to stop, be quiet, and listen.

I have been with you since the day you were born and I will greet you when you return. Right now though, I am wondering where you are.

-Jesus

HEAR ME

*C*lose your eyes now, relax and listen.

What do you hear? You say that you hear nothing.

Listen again. Hear the whispers in your heart. Hear me. Empty your mind for this is meditation. Meditation is listening. I want you to relax because I want to be with you. I want to talk with you.

I want you to see how beautiful life is. Life can always be beautiful. Take a deep breath and saturate yourself in this beauty. Now, let go; give yourself to me. I am here to hold you. I am here to comfort you. Tell me your worries. Tell me your successes. Stay quiet so you can feel my presence and feel my love.

Now, go a little deeper in your relaxation. In the beautiful garden, or seaside, or mountain or valley scene in your mind, can you hear me? I am trying to come through to you. I know you are feeling my presence now but can you hear me?

Relax and take your time. Picture me in your mind. Ask me for messages. They will come to you in your thoughts. Follow your thoughts. As you do this meditation regularly, you will hear my words more clearly. I want you to know that I am always with you. I talk to you constantly but you must make time in your life to listen and hear me.

You may ask yourself many times where are your ideas coming from? Try to remember they are all coming from me. When you hear me strongly, you will tell others that you have a great idea and when you carry it out, it works!!! That is why I say, meditate and 'listen', 'listen' to your thoughts, and 'listen' to your ideas, for they are all from me.

I am with you always. I want you to succeed with your life plan. Listening to me and hearing me are two components of spiritual success. Turn inward to me when you are stressed. Turn inward to me when you are successful. See where life is really taking you…are you directing yourself or are you following your written life plan? The only way to know is by listening so that you may truly hear me.

I am here and I am talking. You are there. Are you listening?

Hear me.

-Jesus

LIFE IS GOOD

I hear many negative statements about life on earth and I receive many pleas for help.

But let's concentrate on the positives in life right now. Sit back and evaluate your life and recognize what you have. Life is really good when you stop to think about it.

Now, close your eyes and let me talk to you for a while. Look at your life as it is right now. Look at your life as it was in the past. Look at your life as it may be in the future.

Is your life good now? Did you like it better a few years ago? Are you looking at the future for a better life? Whatever the circumstances, just look at your life as it is right now. What is happening in your life and are you truly happy? What is TRULY happy, you ask. To be truly happy is to be alive within yourself…to be alive within your soul.

That is very heavy, you proclaim…but it is not, really. When you acknowledge your soul, you see yourself for who you really are and that is a child of God. As a child of God, you are given the privileges of heaven.

And how is that, you ask.

You are here to develop your soul to a higher level and move closer to God. You are watched over constantly and given heavenly help. Guardian angels, archangels, and spirit guides help you through your perceived difficult times on earth. You are never alone. We are always with you. These are some of heaven's privileges. So life really is good.

Look around you now and recognize the love of your neighbors, your friends and your family. See their love for you and for each other.

There is a lot of love on earth. It is everywhere and it surrounds you. Look at the smiles on the faces of those you pass on the street. Look at the smiling faces of the children at the playground. Look at the world around you. It is full of love…see it, feel it, and hear it. It is there but you must open your eyes to receive it.

And I say to you, if you walk through life with your eyes closed and your heart afraid to give and receive love…you will never experience the love of God.

You will never experience the goodness of life.

-Jesus

YOUR TRUE SELF

*D*o you ever look in the mirror to truly see yourself?

Have you ever seen your soul? Your soul is your true self.

Don't be afraid of yourself. Recognize all your good qualities. Recognize and accept your personality as seen within your soul. Be proud to show the world your soul, your true self.

So, how do I find my true self, you ask. The real you is your soul. You have grown away from your soul and consequently you have forgotten who you really are. To return to your soul, you must look within yourself, you must look deep within your heart. . Evaluate your life as it is now and evaluate how much love you see within yourself, within your heart. How much masquerading is part of your life? Are you unkind for the sake of attention and then feel badly about your actions when you are alone? Do you walk away from helping others because you might be criticized but deep within your heart, you want to lend a helping hand?

Look at yourself and look deeply into your soul. Your soul is crying because these actions are not what your soul wants for you. Your soul is working very hard to communicate to you. The guilty feelings you have after you have caused hurt or walked away from an opportunity to help another is your soul crying out to you. The guilty feelings you experience represent the real you and the real you is trying to surface.

Let me help you. My angels and I are with you in all aspects of your life. Your soul is buried right now and we are here to help you return to your soul. Call on us. Call on us whenever a guilty feeling arises from one of your actions. Open your heart to us. When you call, we will know that your heart is opening and that you want to change. You want to look at yourself and reunite with your soul. Call on us every day. This will keep your heart open to our help.

Remember that you are here to develop your soul to move closer to God. Evaluate your life and your soul daily.

Call on me. Call on my angels. We are here to help you stay connected with your soul so you may enjoy the presence of God on earth.

-Jesus

LOVE SURROUNDS YOU

*Y*ou seem sad. You seem lonely.

Why, I ask.

I am here for you, but alas, I see you have forgotten.

You are busy, I know, but stop for a moment and look beyond your life's circle. Look at the sky. Look at the trees. Look at the gardens, the flowers, and the grass. Look closely.

There is love swaying in the trees. There is love floating in the clouds. Look at them closely. Can you see the angels? Can you see their wings? They are surrounding you with love and whispering to you. They are telling you that you are never alone.

Listen to the wind blowing through the trees. Listen to its messages. The wind is engulfing you with love. Embrace it. Why do you hesitate? Do you not believe or do you not understand?

Life, I know, is BELIEVED to be difficult, but it is not. Really, it is not. When you accept all the love that surrounds you, life can be very good and life can be very happy.

But I hear you say, what about cancer? What about drug abuse? What about generalized human abuse? Yes, I say, they all exist and they exist for a reason. Accept the difficulties because they exist to advance the soul. You are fixated on human existence. Move on. Rise above and look at your soul.

Love surrounds you. Look around and receive it. I am here with you, always waiting to enter your soul, to enter your life and fill it with joy, hope and love. But you must open your mind to me and open your heart to me.

Do you remember your neighbor or relative or friend who had cancer several times in her lifetime? Do you remember how happy and positive she was with every difficult situation she encountered? You would remark how strong she was and how she received all her bad news with a smile. You admired her but you did not understand how she was able to accept her suffering as she did. She embraced all her difficulties because she received and felt my love and the love of the angels surrounding her. The radiance you saw was her soul.

My love and the love of the angels exist for you also. You may not have physical difficulties, but you may not be truly happy with your life. Think about it. Think about your soul. What is missing?

Your soul needs nurturing. Your soul needs love. With this nurturing and love comes happiness and contentment. Love surrounds you always so reach out, grab it, and make it a part of your daily life.

I am love and I am with you always. Welcome me into your heart. Welcome me into your life. When I am a part of you, you will unknowingly spread my love to all those who cross your path. Now that you are helping to spread my love, take time for yourself. Sit quietly whenever the time permits. Look around and enjoy your surroundings. Smile. Close your eyes and think of me…think of my angels.

Relax and receive our love. Be strengthened by our love.

Know that love surrounds you always.

-Jesus

WHO ARE YOU

*W*ho are you? Have you ever really thought about that? Have you ever wondered who you really are?

Well, you might say…my name is and I live in this neighborhood and I work for a good company.

But, I ask you again…Exactly Who Are You???

You define your life and who you are by what surrounds you physically. But is that the real you? Does your WORK define who you are, or do YOU define who you are?

I want you to look at your life, as it is now. Evaluate it, and ask yourself if you are truly happy within your heart. Are you truly one with yourself?

It really doesn't matter where you work or where you live; what is important is what exists in your heart. Is it love and happiness? Is it boredom, uselessness, or just plain lack of interest in life?

Boredom, uselessness, and lack of interest in life can happen when you detour from your original life plan. Detours may come along but you don't have to follow them. Stay in touch with me because I can help you maneuver around these detours.

Try this exercise…every morning when you open your eyes and before you get out of bed, smile and whisper 'good morning' to me. This makes me very happy and it sets the tone of the day for you. I know WHO you really are. You see yourself in your human form. I see you in your spiritual form.

Now, to see your spiritual form, look inside your heart. Imagine yourself on a deserted island. You are alone on this island and must face the unrest that has been in your heart since you came to earth. There is no one on this island to judge you, no one to analyze you and no one to criticize you except you yourself. You are now looking at your soul. Look closely at your soul for your soul is the real you. Start to feel peace within yourself. As this feeling of peace rises within you, you will begin to feel happiness. Don't question this feeling of happiness…just enjoy it.

Now that you are in a state of peace and happiness, look at yourself. Look at your personality. Your soul is now filled with love. It is filled with love for yourself and love for all other souls. The boredom, uselessness and lack of interest are gone because you are back on your written path. You have gotten around the detours.

You are now seeing your soul. You are seeing who you really are.

You are now seeing yourself as God sees you.

-Jesus

BE WITH ME

I say to you, 'Be with me', and you say, 'of course, I am with you' or you may say 'what are you talking about'?

I am saying make your life present with me.

For example…when you are at work, and you are performing repetitious tasks, just think of me. Remove all passing thoughts from your mind and make me present in your mind. I am asking you to make yourself aware of being with me.

The world is moving fast but right now, I want you to tune into yourself. I want you to look at yourself and turn to me. I know this is hard because there is so much hustle and bustle around you. I hear you say, 'how do I have time for you'? And I say it is easy but often you resist. You ask me to wait a few years until you get through a lot of projects in your life. But I say to you that NOW is when you need me the most.

When you are under a lot of stress at work or at home, turn to me and call my name. Call me by my name as you would call your best friend. I will hear you. I will come to you. But you MUST call my name. Think of me. Visualize my face. I am here for you. The more you call on me, the more I am able to become a part of you.

As you grow closer to me through these exercises, you will experience an overwhelming feeling of calm. This calm will open your heart and mind to help you make wise decisions…decisions that you will be proud of. You see, the more you call on me, the more you make me a part of your life; the more profound your decision-making will be. Always remember that decision-making is a critical part of your soul development.

Come and be a part of me. Let me into your life for I truly want to work with you. Don't shut me out because you are afraid or because you believe you do not have the time.

Be with me now for I want to help you finish your time on earth and return to me with a happy heart.

Make your life present with me.

-Jesus

BE STRONG

$\mathcal{I}$ am here and I am with you but many times you do not recognize me.

I am the voice in the wind. I am the voice in your heart.

You have many choices each day as you experience life. It is sometimes a lot easier, in your eyes, and a lot more enticing to make an unsavory choice instead of the more difficult 'right' choice. You think to yourself that maybe this is the 'road less traveled'. Well, maybe it is and maybe it is less traveled for a reason. Have you ever thought about that?

Have you ever really analyzed a decision that you have made? Did you take that less traveled road and struggle with life without understanding why? You wonder many times what is happening to you as you continue on this path that you have chosen. You truly believe you should be there because it is the challenge you chose…it is the proverbial 'road less traveled'.

But I say to you now, if you find yourself struggling with decisions in your career, your personal life, or your relationships, please stop and stop immediately. Don't make any hasty changes. Just stop and look at yourself. Look at how difficult your life has become when previously it was so easy. Look at how unhappy you are when previously you were very happy. Look at how chaotic your life has become when previously everything always fell easily into place.

Do you think this happened by accident? Do you think that this is just a string of bad luck coming your way? No, it is not. It is due to an unsavory easy decision you made that moved you away from me and away from your written life plan. Think back. Do you remember when you made this decision to change your life, to take a chance and venture into a new realm? I was with you. The angels surrounded you. We sent you many messages with many signs. Think deeply now.

Do you remember the feelings that you had when you were pondering this change in your life? Do you remember that you did not feel comfortable? Those uncomfortable feelings were being sent to you by me and by my angels, but you exercised free will and chose to follow the 'road less travelled'.

Now, does this mean you should avoid all changes in your life? Should you never venture out when a new opportunity comes your way? My answer to those questions is that you need to look and evaluate every opportunity that crosses your path. You must learn how to read these opportunities. Life throws you many curve balls and it is up to you to decide if you should swing or lay off it.

That is where I come in. Remember…I am always here for you. Ask me and I will give you my opinion. You may not like it and you always have free will. I will continue to send you messages and signs to bring you back to me and to bring you back to your written plan.

Life is easy and life is difficult…you and your life choices make it so. Be strong and come to me. Give me the details of your life and the details of the opportunities that are coming to you.

Come to me first when you need to make an important decision in your life. Discuss it with me. Give me the pros and cons, as you perceive an opportunity. Talk to me and then be quiet. When you are relaxed, I will send you my answer. You may not hear it at first especially if it is not what you want but listen again and again. Listen for several days and then make your decision.

Remember, you always have free will. Your decision may not align with my advice but I will honor all of your decisions.

Be strong and keep telling yourself to be strong for that is what you must be to follow my advice especially when your ego is working very hard to control you.

Be strong and be with me.

-Jesus

SADNESS

*W*hy are you so sad?

Sadness is not what life is all about. I don't want anyone on earth to be sad because it is such a difficult feeling. It is a feeling that can take the life out of you. It can make you despondent and feel worthless.

I don't want anyone to experience sadness but I see it happening everywhere on earth. I see the angels trying to intervene but they return to me saying they were shut out. They were pushed away from the hearts of many sad humans.

Look at yourself right now and look into your soul. What is the true reason for your sadness? What are you missing? Do you believe you are lacking material goods? Is it your health? You only mention health and material goods…things that are perceived as needed for your human existence that you believe will make you happy. But, you ask nothing for your soul. Did you know that when your soul is fulfilled and happy, your body is fulfilled and ultimately happy also?

Now, what do I need to fulfill my soul, you ask.

I say you need…love, happiness, peace, and joy. Have you ever thought of these qualities as being needed by you, needed by your soul? I believe that you have not or if you have, it may have been only for a very short time and you didn't know how to bring them into your life. You didn't know how to incorporate them into your soul.

I am here to tell you how to bring happiness into your life. I am here to tell you how love and joy can bring happiness to your soul. All the material goods in the world will never bring you true happiness. You must allow my love into your heart. When you let my love into your heart, you let God into your heart.

Now sit quietly and turn your thoughts to me and to the angels. Relax and give me your fears, your sadness and your stress. The world is holding on to you. You are afraid to let go…but know that I am here to catch you. Fear in your life totally inhibits you from coming to me. Worry is another unnecessary human element. Fear and worry are two feelings that can put a lock on your heart that can prevent you from receiving my love and happiness.

Come to me now for there is always a way. Life is not as helpless as you imagine it to be. Life is full of love. Life is full of opportunities that I send to you. Look for them and use them to your advantage. I want you to be happy. I will do all that is possible to relieve you of your sadness but you must talk to me and give me the reasons for your sad heart. I want to do this for you because I want you to be happy.

As you receive me into your heart, happiness follows immediately. As your heart fills with my happiness, my joy and my love, your life will then become complete and fulfilled.

Please, come to me and experience the true feeling of happiness.

-Jesus

HEAR THE SONG

*H*ave you ever listened to the words of a song? I mean absolutely any song? There are a lot of meaningful words in songs today. There are words of love, rejection, hurt, happiness, triumph, and compassion.

Did you know that I inspired many of these popular songs? Listen carefully and you will hear my words. Listen to the great country singers. Listen to the gospel singers. Listen to the rock singers. This is a great way for me to speak to you.

There are words of love, words of peace, and words of joy. There are words describing struggles that many endure just to find my love. I want you to listen to the words of songs. They go deeper than any conversation. When you first hear one of these songs, you may say it is great. But I want you to listen again. Listen carefully to the song. What are you saying now? It is more than great, you say, it is inspirational. And when you make that statement, you can be assured, the inspiration came from me.

I have many messages to send to you and I try many ways to get your attention. I know you are still experiencing a lot of what the earth offers to you but don't move too far away from me in the process because I have a lot to say. My message is love and you can hear it resonate in the words of songs.

I am with you everywhere. Just turn on your radio or ipod…I am there. Listen. Be quiet because I want you to hear my words. They are words of love. They are words of healing, words of sharing, and words of happiness, words of sadness, and words of loss.

You hear the words. You sing the words but you don't incorporate them into your life. These words will resonate forever. That is why I want you to listen and hear them because they are from me. They are forever.

Now, sit and put on one of my songs. You ask which one and I say the one you play the most. Put it on, be quiet and enter a meditative state. Feel the beat, feel the rhythm and listen to the words. They are coming to you. Do you feel me? Do you feel my love? It is there. Continue listening and continue feeling. It will come to you because it is from me. Think deeply and feel deeply. I am there. When the song is over stay where you are. Be quiet and reflect on what you just heard and how you feel.

NOW can you see that I am everywhere? You probably had no idea I was in the songs that you listen to. But I have to get my messages out to as many people as possible and music is a very viable medium.

When you are at any book and music store look closely at the songs and the artists. Listen to the songs before you buy them and hear me. You will be surprised, I know, but I try to share my messages among all the artists. Many artists know that I am working with them and welcome me. They sing from their heart and that is where I am.

I say to you again…hear the song, hear the words of the song and hear me. Music is such an enjoyable part of life and there I am right in the middle of all the good sounds in life.

Whenever you turn to music, always know that I am talking and singing to you. Come and sing with me.

Receive my music. Receive my love. Receive me.

-Jesus

LOSS

I know life is difficult and it is easy for you to become angry with me. But it is your choices on earth that many times cause your pain. When pain is difficult, I know you forget about me at that moment but I want you to know that I am always here for you.

I have not forgotten you. You have forgotten me. You have replaced me with your pain. I want to reconnect with you. I want you to know that your pain is temporary.

You say you just lost someone who was very close and dear to you and you ask me how this is temporary. I say to you that it IS temporary because you will be reunited later in heaven. But you say that you can't wait for heaven. You say that you miss your loved one now. And I ask you, what have you learned from this passing? I see that this makes you think and that is good. The passing of a child, or anyone close to you is difficult to understand but there is always a reason. First and foremost, it was their time to move on. It was their time to return to us. They fulfilled their life's purpose on earth.

Your goal and everyone's goal on earth is to stay focused. Don't withdraw because you have experienced the loss of a loved one. Come to me and let me help you understand. You need to understand the levels of soul development. All souls on earth have incarnated for a specific reason and for a specific time. This is written in their life plan. You have a written life plan with specific goals that you want to attain on earth before you return to us. It is important that you stay focused on your soul development and not someone else's soul development.

I know you can become distraught when someone close to you returns to us after spending sometimes only a short time on earth. In your mind, you believe that everyone should live many, many years on earth. That is not always the case.

Come and talk to me when you are overwhelmed with feelings of sorrow and loss. Come to me and cry. I understand your emptiness. Cry on my shoulder. Release all your grief to me. Then sit quietly and listen. Listen for my words of comfort. Listen for my words of healing. Listen for my words of understanding. As you receive all of my words and feel my love, feel the love of the soul you are missing. Feel their love. I have brought them to you now so that you will know they are with me. They are happy and filled with God's love. Remember this moment. When sadness and loss try to enter your life again, pull this moment from your heart and call on me to share it with you.

There is much jubilation when a soul returns to us. Make that jubilation a part of you. Celebrate in your heart because you know the soul that left you is now with me and surrounded by angels.

Come to me and let me help you turn your feelings of sadness to feelings of happiness and contentment.

Give me your loss. Give me your sadness.

-Jesus

WHAT IS YOUR POTENTIAL

$\mathcal{I}$ ask you…what is your potential?

And you say…potential for what?

I ask again…what is your potential?

So many times this word, POTENTIAL, is used to describe a person's ability. But look at it on the spiritual side. I see doubt entering your mind with that statement.

There is no 'potential' on the spiritual side, I hear you say…there is only right and wrong. It is as simple as that. Why do you believe that, I ask. Are you not looking to develop your soul while you are here on earth? What about those who have pulled themselves out of very difficult situations and are now devoting their lives to helping others in similar situations? Don't you think that is soul development?

I see you are thinking, and slowly you say 'yes' that is soul development for that person but what has that to do with me? It has a lot to do with you. You say you always make the 'right' choices. You help others whenever you are needed but then you tell the world about it. You boast about all the good deeds you do.

I ask you again…what is your potential?

If you do all these good deeds for the approval of others then where is your reward? As I see it, you want your rewards to come from your fellow workers, your neighbors, and your relatives. Are they a part of your soul development? Will they evaluate your soul as you perform good deeds and give you reward points? NO, they will not. To do your good deeds for the approval of others is empty giving.

Now, look at your life. Are you paying attention to the real reason you help others or are you just performing for approval and praise? Start looking at your life and your actions with regard to your soul. Turn the thoughts of your deeds to the effect and outcome they may have on another. Are you truly affecting and improving their life? If you get no recognition...are you upset?

Extending your hand to those in need for the purpose of helping them and not for your own glory and popularity is soul development. Giving a compliment or helpful comment to a fellow competitor with the expectation of nothing in return is soul development.

Now, I say to you again...what is your potential? Where are you in your soul development process?

As you become aware of your actions, you will see a change in yourself. Be aware of how you feel. Do you feel an inner peace? Do you feel an inner calm?

Life should be a joy to you and not a chore. Performing for the sake of approval is always chore.

Remember as you develop your soul on earth you will reach your full potential of truly seeing the glory of God.

-Jesus

NEED ME

*L*ook within yourself. Are you searching for something? Are you searching for me? I am always with you. I surround you. I am with the angels who surround you. They are constantly sending you messages from me...can you hear them?

You are busy, I know, but when you take some quiet time, listen and you will hear their voices. They are guiding and protecting you. And it is I who is sending them to you.

When life is good to you and everyone around you is happy, you believe there is no need for me to be in your life. But that can be very deceiving. Life is full of difficulties and you never know when one will enter your life.

When you come upon a difficulty or catastrophe in life, you usually turn to my angels or me for help and guidance. I know that you need me at these times because I hear you calling me for help. But why don't you think of calling me when your life is good? You believe you do not need me in good times. You have been conditioned to call me primarily when your life becomes difficult or presents you with a catastrophe.

I hear you say that you DO believe I am with you in good times but you feel you don't have to communicate with me as you do in difficult times. And I say...why not?

Have you ever thought to say 'thank you' for your good life, 'thank you' for your health and 'thank you' for your friends and family? When you talk to me, I can feel when your heart is truly happy.

When we have a constant dialogue, help comes to you more easily when a difficulty arises because you are already open to receiving me and receiving my angels. This is what my angels and I truly want to do…we want to make life as easy as possible for you.

Now do you think you need me?

Think about it.

-Jesus

RHYTHMS OF LIFE

*W*hen you hear the distant roar of thunder as a storm approaches, you become alert.

You look towards the sky for warnings from the darkening clouds.

Do the clouds look ominous? Are they dark and heavy? Or do they look to be far away and moving slowly?

Whatever the situation, you are aware. You quietly make a mental note of when you should leave the area and where you can take shelter.

Now, the thunder of the approaching storm is not the danger. Lightning is the danger and thunder is the warning. You get warnings, you take action and then you are safe. It is easy and it works.

Nature is like that. There is calm weather, followed by warnings from thunder and wind and then the storm appears. After the storm, it is calm again. It is a rhythm. Your life is a rhythm. What is the rhythm of life, you say. The rhythm of life is the flow of your life with everyday experiences. You arise in the morning and prepare for your day. Most of the time all goes well for you. You are comfortable with your routine. This is the calm rhythm. Look at the calm rhythm in your life and enjoy it.

Now one day you may get a disturbing message. This message warns you of trouble coming into your life. You react alarmingly to the news but you shrug it off because you don't feel any urgency with the message. This is the warning rhythm.

Now, another warning sign comes to you. Again you ignore it. You may even get a third warning sign. You are now living in the warning rhythm of your life.

Suddenly, your health begins to deteriorate or there is turmoil in your relationships. This is the beginning of the storm rhythm entering your life. Now, how big is this storm and how long will it last? That is up to you because only you control your life's rhythms.

Look at your life right now. Are you in a calm rhythm, a warning rhythm or a storm rhythm? Identify your rhythm. Are you happy with what you see? This is a very important question. For in this answer you will identify where you stand with God and with yourself.

If you are in the calm rhythm of your life take time to identify with your soul. The calm rhythm is a good time to unite with God. It is a good time to strengthen your relationship with Him because it is this relationship with God that will carry you through the storm rhythms of your life. Always remember there will be a calm rhythm following a storm rhythm but it is up to you to turn to God to guide you through the storms. I know you have many doubts about this analysis because the storms can be very brutal and dark but know that I am always with you.

So I say to you now take a deep breath if you are in a storm rhythm and all seems hopeless to you. Find some quiet time and ask the angels to come and walk with you. Stay quiet and feel their presence. You will feel peace because the angels are renewing your strength. Use this feeling of strength and love to help carry you through your storm and into the calm rhythm of your life.

The rhythms of life are always with you. Recognize them.

-Jesus

WHO ARE YOU

*H*ave you ever wondered who you really are?

Have you ever wondered why you are here on earth?

Have you ever wondered what life is all about?

These are difficult questions. They are difficult because you can't actually see the development of your soul and that is what these questions relate to.

Material success does not necessarily translate into spiritual success. You may have had a very happy childhood. You may have a very successful life right now but is that who you really are? You shake your head yes because you say you worked very hard to get where you are today. Now, if you don't view yourself as successful, do you feel you have been given a bad rap and that you never had a chance to move on to succeed in life? Look at yourself again…successful or not is this who you really are? Have you ever thought… is this all there is to life?

I hear many cries for help to change a situation in life. I also get many 'thank you' messages for a comfortable life. I still ask, successful or not…is this truly who you are? If you are happy, are you truly happy or just happy because you are comfortable with your surroundings? If you are angry or depressed…is it because of your health or position in life? These are all earthly effects you are experiencing but they do not define you. Your soul defines you.

To examine your soul closely, you must look within yourself. I see you have no idea how to do that and you are afraid. You feel it might reveal too much of yourself to you. You are worried that if you look deeply at your soul you may not like what you see. But knowing your 'soul' self is truly a rewarding experience. Your soul is here to learn. It is here to experience as much of life as possible.

How you receive life's experiences may be a reflection of your soul. If you believe you are happy but not complete, your soul is calling you to open your heart to receive my love. If you struggle with worry, anxiety or depression, then your soul is yearning for you to open to me to help you understand your life, and to help you to love yourself.

Your soul is who you really are.

You say to me…'how can I find my soul'? It is easy but you must be patient because in your busy world there are many distractions. First, you must make a commitment to yourself to open your mind and heart to receive my angels and me. We are here for your entire lifetime on earth.

In your quiet times, just think of me and ask me to come into your life. Do this as often as you can and do it until it becomes a part of you. As you become stronger through me, you will start to see the world differently. The world and all that is happening in your life will become more meaningful. You will then begin to see your soul. You will begin to see who you really are.

Don't let the true meaning of your life on earth pass you by.

-Jesus

WHISPERS

*H*ave you ever heard the wind talk to you?

Have you ever heard the ocean or the mountains whisper special messages to you?

You are shaking your head yes but you are thinking they were just sounds that your mind made into words and that is partly true. They are sounds made into words but my angels and I are the ones making them into words that you can understand.

Why, you ask, why are you doing that?

We are trying to communicate with as many people as possible. We are saying there is a tremendous amount of love, peace, and joy flowing onto earth, even now as you read this. We seize every opportunity to send our love to earth in the hope that it will be received and spread.

Listen to the wind as it gently blows through the trees. Stop as you are walking and look at the trees. Feel the wind. Feel my love and hear my words. Know that I am walking with you and talking to you. The angels are with you also and sending you many signs. Look around you. Are the clouds long and wispy like angel wings? Look at them and be happy for they are signs from the angels signaling they are walking with you also.

Are you near the ocean, a river, or even a small stream? Stand still and look deeply into the water. What do you see? Nothing, you answer. Look again. The colors of the water swirl around your reflection. Stay there.

We are with you surrounding you with love. We are whispering words of love, peace, and joy to you. Recognize us in the swirling water and receive these feelings.

You ask…why are you sending all these messages that many are oblivious to receiving? That is because we do not give up easily. We continue and will always continue to send God's messages of love, peace and joy to the earth no matter how many people look past them. Because the earth is a difficult environment, we surround you with angels and love.

Sit quietly and look around you…look for me and look for the angels. It takes practice. Go for a walk and look at the trees, at the flowers, and even at the grass. If you see them move or sway in the wind…think of me. This is how you start to tune in to our signs. Did a feather just cross your path? You say there are a lot of birds in the area. That may be true but did you ever pay attention to a feather landing just in front of your next step? We directed your eyes to that feather to let you know we are with you. It is up to you to acknowledge the feather and recognize that this as a sign from us. We are walking with you. It is not hard to tune into us and see and hear us.

It is up to you to open your eyes and heart to see me. I am in the wind. I am in the clouds. I am in the mountains. I am in the ocean. See me and see yourself. If you spend just one day with these elements, you will spend the rest of your life on earth with me.

I say to you now…will you receive the wind? Will you receive me? Or will you just let the wind blow through your hair as you look blindly at the trees and grass and go on with your life?

Always remember…I love you.

-Jesus

DO YOU REMEMBER

*L*et's go down memory lane.

Do you remember as a child you always knelt beside your bed to say goodnight to me and goodnight to your guardian angels?

Do you remember falling down and scraping your knee or arm and your mom kissing your injury and telling you not to cry because God would make it better?

Do you remember sitting down to dinner with your family and asking God to bless your food?

Do you remember saying a million prayers to my angels and me just before a big test in school?

Do you remember hiding under the covers during a thunderstorm with your mother / father who told you not to be afraid because the thunder was only the angels having fun at the bowling alley?

Think about your childhood. You were always told to give all your major worries and fears to God and to your guardian angels. Your parents guided you to me and to the angels in every aspect of your life.

What happened?

You grew up and you started to drift away from my angels and me. Your requests for our help became fewer and fewer. You reached your teen years. These were difficult years, because you were looking to find yourself. Sometimes you remembered to call on the angels and me but that was mostly for a big sport event or a big test. I'm not knocking that. In fact the angels and I were happy you called on us because that showed us that we were still a part of your life.

Then, you graduated high school and moved on with your life. You were very busy then. The angels and I, who were once a major part of your life, stayed quiet waiting for you to return to us. As you progressed, life got a little more complicated and there were many decisions to make. But, you seemed happy with yourself and the decisions you were making about your life. You settled into a routine of work and having fun. You were enjoying your new state of independence.

Then, you visited one of your friends who had a little child. You stood in the doorway and watched the parents guide their child through his nighttime prayers. You had a flashback of yourself kneeling before your bed and reciting the same prayers. We were happy because we saw the window to your soul open slightly. We knew it would be slow because there was still a lot you wanted to experience in life and you wanted to do it on your own. We wanted to tell you that talking with us once in a while would be okay. We would not take your independent decision-making away from you. We would just give you some guidance, if you asked for it, and then it would be your choice to accept or reject our advice.

Now, you have children of your own. Their rooms are decorated with teddy bears and angels. Do you remember your room as a child?

You teach your little children to say goodnight to God. Do you remember saying goodnight to God?

Your children jump into your bed at the first sound of thunder and you tell them about the angels at the bowling alley. Do you remember your angels bowling?

Your children grow to adults and you see how they have drifted away from the angels and from God. Do you remember this pattern with yourself? Can you see the pattern repeating yet?

Do you remember your feelings when you knew the angels were surrounding you?

Return to those feelings.

Return to the angels.

-Jesus

ANGER

$\mathcal{D}$o you lose your temper easily?

Are you quick to judge others?

Do friends come in and out of your life?

Do you believe other people are always at fault and not you?

Why do you believe you always have the right answer, or the right opinion and that everyone else is wrong? Are you sure about your answers and opinions? Can they be documented well enough to justify belittling another person to the point that they want to crawl into a hole? Now think…would YOU like to be put down this way? Would you like to be on the receiving end of one of YOUR tirades?

Close your eyes and evaluate your life right now. I am sure you are seeing yourself as a calm and rational person. Think and visualize the last time you were stopped by a police officer for a traffic violation. How angry were you? Did your knuckles become white gripping the steering wheel? Did you bang the steering wheel when the officer gave you the speeding ticket? Now, you know, he was justified for his actions. It was YOU who was reacting because you believe you are the perfect one. You believe no one has the right to interfere with your actions and decisions.

Please, stop right now. Close your eyes and look into your heart. Your heart is crying. It is crying and you are not hearing it. You are not seeing its tears. Look deep into your heart. Look to see how empty it is. It is empty of true love. It is empty of God's love. You are trying to fill it but you don't know what to fill it with. So you are filling it with anger.

One should never continually keep anger in their heart. It will not only destroy you physically but it will continue to grow inside you. As it grows larger inside you, your life will become increasingly difficult. I say to you now that unless you remove all anger from your heart and replace it with love, you will be forever without God. God does not exist in angry environments. God does not exist in the turmoil of hate.

Remove your anger and return to love.

Return to God.

-Jesus

HAPPINESS

*H*appiness is a state of mind. It is a state of the heart. It is a state of feeling.

Are you happy? Do you experience feelings of happiness and love?

Happiness is a feeling that I want everyone to experience on earth. Happiness is everywhere but you may not see it. Sometimes happiness is hidden because the earth has many sad events. You must look past them. You can't dwell on sadness and negative events. They happen and they are a part of life.

Look for the little things in life and enjoy them. Go for a walk. Breathe the fresh air and feel how it refreshes your lungs. Be happy because you are not only breathing fresh air but you are also outside communing with nature. Walk. Walk with vigor and fill your heart with happiness… for the angels and I are with you. Look for us in the sky. Look for us in the wind. Look for us in the smiles of those whom you pass.

You say that you don't have time to walk or enjoy any outdoor activity… but I want you to find the happiness that surrounds you. You say… IMPOSSIBLE and I say… POSSIBLE!

So I ask you…why do you believe it is impossible? Recognize negative statements that may surround you and counter them with positive ones. If people do not want to hear the good side of life then just walk away from them. That will be the beginning of your return to me and your return to happiness.

When you are stuck in heavy traffic, I say to you…relax. Use this time to tune into me. Think of me as your passenger and talk to me. Tell me what you have planned for the day. Tell me your frustrations. Don't just think these thoughts; verbally talk to me about them. Over time you will enjoy driving in heavy traffic at a snail's pace because you know this is an opportunity to talk with me. This is a time for me to help you open your heart to God. When your heart opens to God, it fills with happiness and love.

Everyone should be happy on earth but many resist opening their hearts. You can help by spreading YOUR happiness. Spread your happiness and your feelings of joy, to your friends, family and strangers.

I am happiness and happiness is you because you are a part of me.

-Jesus

ARE YOU THERE

I have been calling your name but there is no answer.

Where are you? Are you there?

I see you are busy with your life, with your friends, and with your family. But when did you forget me?

I was always part of your life when you were young. I was even part of your life when you were a young teen. But as you finished school and went out on your own, you stopped talking to me. I know you did not forget me but I became a shadow in your life.

Your soul is being deprived. It is being pushed aside to satisfy your human needs. Taking care of your soul is easy but it is always the first to be cast aside. I watch the patterns that souls follow as they drift away from me. Souls start searching as teenagers to define themselves and they tend to move away from me because they don't think it is 'cool' to say the words 'prayer' or 'meditation' or 'angel' or even 'God'. These are difficult years to transition through so angels always surround souls in their teenage years sending them love, messages and signs.

As souls move through their twenties and thirties, communication with the angels or me is still usually very low. I watch how you are developing your human psyche and establishing your position on earth. I see you are successful now and you are very happy. That is good because everyone here in heaven wants you to be happy and fulfilled on earth. I call out to you many times during this period of your life but you don't hear me. I keep asking…'are you there, can you hear me'? There is no answer.

Now you are in your forties and fifties. The world around you is suddenly changing. You see friends and acquaintances moving out of secure employment positions due to corporate upheavals. You see families breaking apart. You begin to see sickness and death. What is this, you say? My perfect world is starting to shake. But I am here with you. I am trying to explain everything to you. You do not hear me. I keep calling…'are you there, please let me in'.

You continue on with life observing the many tragedies around you. I see you absorbing the intensity of these tragedies…a parent or sibling with cancer, the sudden death of a very good friend, or the demise of a relative due to drug abuse. You watch intently but you still don't turn to me.

So again, I ask, where are you? Why don't you answer? I want to be a part of your life on earth and help you.

So please, when I call, don't hang up. Pick up my thoughts and let me into your life.

I am here for you. My angels are here for you.

Will you answer? Are you there?

-JESUS

LISTEN TO ME

'*Listen* to me'…how many times have you heard that phrase?

The first time, I am sure, was from your parents as they were guiding you through life as a young child. They wanted only the best for you. They didn't want you to make the same mistakes they had made in their lives. They wanted to spare you some of the pain they experienced. So you would hear the phrase 'listen to me'. But, of course, you didn't listen because you wanted to experience life yourself.

Many times, I say to you, 'listen to me' and you turn away. You don't hear me. I believe you don't WANT to hear me. This is your free will exerting its power. However, I would like to show you a little of what I can do to help you. Remember, I am not entering into your life and I am not demanding that you follow me in a certain way. I am just trying to help you make the best decisions in your life…choices that will benefit your soul. Even when you exercise free will and make a choice on your own, I am with you. I am with you to walk you through any decision, be it good or bad that you choose.

I am here for you, giving you signs and messages. I know you probably think my advice is like your parents' advice and you just want to scream…'I WANT TO DO IT MYSELF'. I am here to tell you to live your own life. I want you to follow what you feel in your heart. But only when you learn to really listen to your heart will you begin to hear me.

I speak to you through your heart. I am the voice that you feel. I am the good feeling that you have throughout your body. Start paying attention to those feelings. If you routinely dismiss them you will miss many good opportunities in life.

I hear you now asking…how do I REALLY hear from you? An easy way to learn to hear me is to sit quietly a few times a week and empty your mind. Ask me if there are any messages for you. After a few minutes, thoughts will enter your mind regarding a situation you are worried about. Receive those thoughts because they are my thoughts. After you do this several times, you will become conditioned to hearing me. You will hear and feel me in your heart daily. So, when I say, 'listen to me', I am asking you to open your heart, hear my words, and receive my love for you.

Life is much easier when you welcome me into your heart.

Listen to me.

-JESUS

LIFE

*H*ave you ever thought what life is all about?

Have you ever thought about who you really are?

Have you ever thought about your place in the world?

Do you ever think about other people in the world or do you stay focused in your world, close to your home?

Do you ever think about the order of the universe…the sun, the moon, and possibly how the universe is governed?

These are questions that humans have thought and philosophized about for centuries.

Now, I want you to look within yourself when you ask the question… 'who am I and why am I here'? Are you looking at your immediate environment and your possessions for your answer? Why do you think they define you? You are only looking at yourself through human eyes. Human eyes can see only human development.

Close your eyes and sit quietly. Look at yourself. Look inside yourself. How is your heart? Is it happy? Does your heart like to share good news? Does it like to share love and kindness? You say you are happy but not all the time. There is absolutely no reason to be unhappy when you are looking at your soul. I ask you again, what are you looking at? Are you looking at your soul or your body?

You say you are trying to look at your soul to find a smile within yourself but it is hard. And I say to you again, LOOK at your soul. Look real hard. Remove all the human negative elements from the thoughts that are pulling you down.

The soul is here to experience good times as well as difficult times. Now look at YOUR soul. Accept the difficulties along with the happiness in your life because they are both advancing your soul.

So, when a difficulty or illness or disability crosses your path, be it long term or short term, don't feel sorry for yourself. Look at your soul and be happy because this is an opportunity to move closer to God. As your soul moves closer to God, your whole being moves into happiness.

And that is what life is all about. Life is about your soul

-JESUS

MEDITATION

$\mathcal{M}$editation.

What a thought provoking word.

It is a word that is increasing in popularity. People feel proud to announce they meditate every morning or evening. It is the 'in' thing to do today.

But do they really know what true meditation is?

Do they meditate long enough to clear their minds in order to receive messages from my angels and messages from me? Do they even know they will be receiving messages from us? Do they dismiss our messages thinking they are from their own mind? This is what the new meditative craze has brought to surface.

To begin, know that true meditation is hearing from my angels and me and that is why you quiet your mind from your thoughts of the world. The first time you meditate, many thoughts from your day will surface. Do not dwell on a thought…dismiss it immediately.

At the end of the session you may feel like you are getting nowhere. You ask yourself…why am I doing this? It is too hard. But know that if you haven't relaxed and quieted your mind in thirty, forty, or even fifty years, why do you think you can quiet it completely in half an hour? This process takes time.

When you have learned to quiet your mind, don't LOOK for messages to come through to you…just let them happen. Remember, meditation is God and the angels talking to you and not you talking to them.

As you continue to meditate, your mind will learn to relax and it will relax to a deeper level. It is at this deeper level that we are able to communicate with you. We send small messages and feelings to see if you are receiving our energy. When we see that you are receiving our information we will increase our energy to send you more specific messages.

When you become aware of messages you may think they are from yourself. You may think it is your mind talking to you. But listen carefully to the message, analyze it and if you feel love with the words of the message, then know it is from us. Sometimes the angels just want to surround you with peace and love with no specific message. When they do, you will feel an exhilarating tingle travel along your spine and a joyous feeling in your heart. Stay there and enjoy the peaceful moment.

Remember, meditation is not just to lower your blood pressure, or your anxiety…it is a means to connect with my angels and with me. By connecting with us through meditation, you are raising your awareness of me in your every day experiences.

So, jump on the bandwagon and meditate. It will be strange at first. But know you are progressing closer to me. My arms are outstretched to receive you. Once you touch them you will never want to let go. I am waiting for you.

I am your meditative thought.

-JESUS

SAFETY

$\mathcal{D}$o you know what safety is?

I know most of you will answer that safety is the protection of yourself and your environment from outside intruders.

You say you are safe. But, I say, what are you safe from? When you ask me for safety for your family, exactly what are you asking for? There is safety for their bodies, safety for their possessions and even safety for their psyches…but do you ever ask for safety for their soul? Do you ever ask for safety for your own soul?

The soul is a precious commodity, yet there are very few requests for its protection. Ah! I hear you asking…exactly what kind of protection is necessary for the soul? Isn't it self-sufficient? Doesn't it just go along with the body? And my answer is…no and no.

The soul needs protection from the many detours in life that work to move the soul away from God. The soul is self-sufficient but it is subject to your free will. The soul goes along with the body but it is NOT the body. The body is your engine on earth and your soul uses your body to experience life on earth. Your soul will return to me and report its experiences with your body. Your body will NOT return or report to me.

Can you see what I am saying?

Do you see why you should be asking for protection for your soul? Asking for protection for your soul is asking for protection for your body. As you tend to your soul, you will tend to your body. Now, go inside and go to your soul. Release any hurt or worries or pain to me. Release your soul and release your pain. Set up a safety net for your soul and free your body of unnecessary burdens.

I see you still do not understand the relationship of the body with the soul.

The body and the soul are one. They work in unison. The soul receives the body for the purpose of experiencing life on earth. It is through the body's experiences that the soul is able to grow, mature and move closer to God. So the soul takes on the body as an employer takes on an employee. The employee does all the work and the employer receives the results…be they good or bad. If the employee (the body) performs poorly then the employer (the soul) will not progress spiritually as planned.

So when you think of asking for safety, think first for the safety of your soul. Ask that your soul be protected from interfering outside sources and be guided by the angels and archangels to stay within God's realm.

Always remember, your soul returns to me. Your body does not return to me.

I am your safety net.

-JESUS

LOVE ME

o You Love Me?

I hear you answer yes, but many times I wonder. I try to talk to you, but you do not answer. I send you many signs with the angels but, again, you do not respond.

Life on earth can be very complex and because of your fast pace, I see you are taking very little time for your soul.

Let me give you something to think about. Do you know why you are on earth? You are on earth to develop your soul and your soul ONLY.

I am looking at you right now and I see that you are very busy with your life and it seems that you have forgotten me. You say that you go to church frequently and you feel that is sufficient. But is that all you want from me? Let me tell you…you are missing the boat. You are missing an abundance of spiritual help and love. Spiritual help is my direct assistance to you. And without this spiritual help, it is very easy to drift away from me.

So, I ask you again…do you love me? Tell me loud and clear that you love me. Those words are very strong. If you realize the power of saying the words, 'Jesus - I love you', you would be shouting them loud and clear all day long, every day of the year.

By telling me that you love me, you are also saying that you need me and you welcome me into your heart. When that happens, your whole world will start changing. You will be happy even though you still have the same worries and fears. You will look at them differently and instinctively know that your life is on a new path. Love me and 'the world is yours'…as the expression goes. It is true. Try it. Whisper my name and tell me you love me. Watch how everything around you starts changing.

Love me as I love you.

Walk with me as I walk with you.

-JESUS

KINDNESS

*Y*ou know the old saying…'Do unto others as you would have done unto you'.

You say it, but do you practice it?

Think about it. When someone cuts you off as you are driving, what is your first reaction? You WANT to step on the gas and cut this person off in retaliation. 'Do unto others as you would have done unto you'. Now I ask you…is speeding and cutting this person off with your car, what you would want done to you? I don't think so. Because this happened, think of it as a test. Should you react and do the same to them in return or should you stop and think for a second, and tell yourself that you don't like what just happened but you will not return the action?

True kindness comes from the heart. It comes from the soul.

You walk down the street and see a handicapped person or child. Do you recoil and whisper 'thank you' that you do not have the difficulties of that person? Or do you look at that person or child and marvel at how they are dealing with their difficulties. Kindness would inspire you to approach that person, say hello and smile from your heart when you can see they are hurting both physically and mentally.

So, please, be kind. Be kind when you get an irritable customer service assistant who cuts you off in mid-sentence. Stop before you react and try to understand their actions. You are ready to attack them because YOUR needs are not being met, but remember… 'Do unto others as you would have done unto you'. Think, would you like to have someone verbally attack you? The answer is overwhelmingly NO. So if you don't want to be verbally attacked, why do you verbally attack someone else?

Be kind. It will get you everywhere.

Those who are nasty to you usually have other difficult situations occurring in their lives. It is up to you to recognize that. By being kind to those who are unkind to you will bring a ray of sunshine into their day. Your day will feel complete because you know you just made a positive impact on someone who was having a 'bad' day.

Bring forth your kindness and give it to the world. Think of the world as you know it now and picture how the earth would be if every human reached deep inside their heart and brought forth their own kindness. There would be no more anger. There would be no more hatred. There would be no more jealousy and there would be no more violence.

Take advantage of the opportunities that arise that would help you become aware of extending your kindness. Work with me. I will help you to be kind when you have difficulty pulling it from your heart.

I am kindness. Make me a part of you and kindness will become a part of you.

Remember...kindness is in your heart. I am in your heart.

By making me a part of your life, you are bringing kindness into your life.

-JESUS

WHY ME

*W*HY ME, Lord?

You hear this expression many times. It is often heard when a person is presented with some very disturbing news such as a severe injury or illness. Their loudest cry is...WHY ME??? What did I do to deserve this?

I say to those who cry out...you did nothing to deserve this EXCEPT that you are a very strong soul who can handle what has just been handed to you. Sure, it is difficult. Sometimes it appears that it is beyond difficult but I want you to look beyond the hardship handed to you. I want you to look to me. I want you to look to the angels. We are here to help you move through difficult times in your life.

I often hear the statements...why does this have to happen? WHY ME?

It has to happen because it is a part of life on earth. Hardships grow the soul. Hardships force you to go inward to search your soul. Many of you blame current hardships on past errors you may have committed in your life. That is not true. God does not have a retribution list as many humans think. Difficulties on earth are written for only very strong souls. When these souls recognize and accept what they have written, they are on their path to developing their soul...they are moving closer to God.

Have you ever visited a children's hospital for cancer? I can feel your trepidation now. Fear and sorrow surround you. Fear is for you and sorrow is for the children. But as you approach each ward, you hear giggling and screams of laughter. The children have accepted their lives.

They are not afraid. Their parents are afraid. Their parents are afraid of losing their child. And that is understandable. But go back to the children. This is THEIR life. They are not in their rooms moaning... WHY ME. They are making new friends. They are making the best of their life, as they know it. Watch them. Learn from them. They are growing their souls.

So when a hardship comes your way and you immediately think...WHY ME? I say to you...'Why not you'? Remember to call out to me and say...'Why me, Jesus'? Then tell me what you don't understand about what you are experiencing. I will explain all that is happening to you in your life and why.

But there is a catch. You must be quiet and listen carefully and accept all that I say to you. You may not agree with what you hear and you may argue with me, but I will guide you through all of your life's difficulties. When you open up to receive my help you will become aware of the presence of angels surrounding you. They surround you to bring you comfort, love and guidance.

This is an important life lesson for you to understand. Always know that you are never alone while experiencing any of life's difficult lessons.

Know you are always surrounded by love.

You are surrounded by my love.

-Jesus

LOOK AROUND

*L*ook around you. What do you see?

You say that you see nothing in particular.

But I say to you again…look around you. Are there trees, mountains, oceans, wooded areas, neighborhood streets, manicured lawns, crowded city sidewalks or lonely country roads?

Whatever you see, don't look past it. Look at what is in front of you and absorb it because I am there in whatever you see.

How do I see you on a dirty, crowded city street, you ask. I say again, look, and look hard because I am there. I am with all the people who rush by you on the sidewalks…I am with the vendors, I am with the people who appear to have nothing, and I am with the tourists and city workers.

Yes, I am there but you do not see me.

Look at the traffic and the traffic lights. Without the traffic lights, the flow of traffic would be chaotic. Now, insert me into the equation. You see, traffic lights are there for a reason. They provide safety and guidance. Now think of what I do in your life. I provide safety and guidance. I am here for your soul development just as safety measures are in place for your human development. I want you to become aware of your surroundings. I want you to connect the world you live in with the spiritual world.

To receive me, you first must look for me, then you must recognize me, and finally, you must welcome me into your life. Look for me in all parts of your life. You may think that by recognizing me, you automatically welcome me into your life. That is not always true. Many people will recognize me but then deny me. Recognize me and consciously welcome me into your life.

Don't give up looking around you and looking for me. Your eyes WILL open because you are consciously working to bring me into your life. You will see me and when you do your life will change. You will see beauty all around you no matter where you are.

You are never too busy to look around at your environment and you should NEVER be too busy to work on your soul. As you move through life, remember, your soul is as important as your body. Many believe the body is on earth to experience life and the soul is second fiddler. But know that the soul is with the body to experience life on earth. The body will end and the soul will continue on.

So, doesn't it make sense to take care of your soul a little more than you do? I am here for you. My angels are here for you. All you have to do is look around to see us and then connect with us. You are not alone on earth even though you might think you are.

Remember, your soul continues on…care for it now.

Think about that and look around. Look for me.

-Jesus

LIFE IS FUN

$\mathcal{L}$ife is fun.

Trust me, it is fun. And it should be fun.

You have many distractions and difficulties that come your way so I know that you sometimes forget to enjoy life. But really, it is fun and it is enjoyable.

If you keep waiting for the 'big break' to occur where you will inherit millions of dollars and think that will make you happy because you could do anything you want with money...think again. Money does not grow on trees, happiness does.

I see you frowning and laughing now. How does happiness grow on trees, you ask. Well, think about it. Many trees blossom in the spring to give enjoyment and happiness to all those who cross their path. Some trees, by their size alone, bring happiness to those who stand near them enjoying their majesty and beauty. And then there is the Christmas tree...the evergreen so revered in the winter months and decorated by many in the Christmas season. It is truly a sign of joy and happiness.

I still hear you saying...HOW CAN LIFE BE FUN? It can be fun by the way you look at it, I say.

Yes, there are terrible things happening everywhere on earth but they have been occurring since the beginning of time. I don't want you to think of that right now. The angels and I are monitoring violence and hardships on earth very closely. So leave that job to us.

So, I say to you, enjoy life…it really CAN be fun.

Look at each moment in YOUR life. Walk your neighborhood. See the children playing, laughing and having a really good time. Look at them closely. I want you to remember when you were a child. Remember how you laughed. Remember how you loved vacations with your family? You always laughed and had a great time. Now, as an adult, I want you to laugh again. I want you to look at life and really enjoy it. You are on earth for a very short time, please do not spend the majority of your time fretting about tomorrow.

Give your worries to me. Trust me. I will help you with whatever is bothering you, but the secret is to give them to me and that, my friend, is the secret to having fun in life!

I am sure you have seen individuals who are experiencing difficulties in their lives and yet, you see them smiling. They are laughing and telling YOU jokes. They are the ones who have accepted their life because they know we are with them every step of the way. They have no worries with their difficulties. They have given everything to us. I see a big frown on your face now. How can this be, I see you thinking. Well, it is because they believe in me and trust in me. If you do not believe or trust in me then you cannot laugh the true laugh of a child.

So come. Come to me. Come to my angels. Life on earth is way too short to be worried, afraid and depressed about tomorrow. Stay in the present time, enjoy it, nourish it, and by all means…have fun.

I want to see you laugh again. I want to see you laugh your childhood laugh and not your adult semi-real laugh. Laugh from your belly. Look at your family and friends and smile…smile a truly genuine smile from your heart. It will look good and it will make you feel good.

Think about all that I have said here and meditate on it. Life offers many opportunities...grab them while you can and enjoy them.

Enjoy life.

Enjoy me.

-Jesus

THE FLOW OF LIFE

$\mathcal{T}$here is a flow of life on the spiritual level. I am sure that you have never thought about it, or experienced it.

The flow of life is driven forward by love and positive happenings in your life. The flow of life is stopped when negative actions and thoughts enter your life.

I sense you are struggling with this.

I want you to think of all the negative thoughts that you may have had today. Think about the moment you reacted to the employee who said your request could not be honored because a manager was unavailable. Your temper started to percolate. With your temper rising and negative thoughts coming to you, the flow of life stood still.

Yes, you can stop the natural flow of life. Negative thoughts, words, and actions bring the flow of life to a complete stop.

How can this be, you ask, because you feel you are just standing up for your rights as a person? The answer is contained in HOW you project 'your perceived rights'. Sure, you want what is right for you and even for your neighbor, but when you use an attack statement, everything in life stands still. There is no reaction because life cannot react to negativism. It can only stop.

That is why you receive virtually nothing when you DEMAND results. Life does not respond to demands. You believe the employee is blocking you and stopping your request but that is not true. Their persona is literally stopped because you made a demand and stopped their flow of life. You believe they are not capable in their position but again that is not true. You are the one who caused the difficulty, not them. You stopped the flow of life, not them.

The flow of life is beautiful and miraculous. Yes, I said 'miraculous'. How can that be, I hear you say. Look at history in all parts of the world. In the middle of a major war, soldiers in field trenches from opposite sides came together at Christmastime on a battlefield and offered each other a drink in the name of peace. For a short period of time, all the negative forces of war stopped, the positive energy flowed and the enemies came together in love. The flow of life is truly able to 'Move Mountains'.

My angels and I will guide you to fill your life with positive energy and let the flow of life become a part of you. Many people will tell you that they like to be around you. They say it just 'feels good' to be near you. Go with this positive energy you are projecting and let it grow.

Remember, the flow of life is contagious. People want it more than the unrest that exists in life but they don't know they can just reach out and it will be theirs.

It all starts with one person. Let that one person be you. Working together with me, we can create a flow of love in life that is so powerful that it can reach the ends of the earth.

Be that Flow of Love.

Be the Flow of Life.

-Jesus

DECISIONS

*L*ook at your life now. How do you rate it? How are you doing with your human goals at work, at home, with family and friends?

How are you doing spiritually? That's a zinger, isn't it?

How many articles do you read about your spiritual health? Think about that! You say that all is going well for you... so, what else is there to deal with in life? And I say, your soul of course. And you say,...that's true but not right now because I am too busy. This is the best time to think of your soul. It is when you are the busiest that you need me the most.

You are so involved with your life on earth and developing your human needs that you are totally forgetting about your soul. When did soul development take a back seat to human development? I know life on earth is difficult but it is the soul that must be nurtured before the body because the soul continues long after the human body ceases to exist.

Human needs are a great priority on earth. Human needs are extremely important for success in life. But what is success in life without success on the soul level? And exactly what is 'soul success', I hear you ask. Soul success is the success that you have at the human level with your soul.

Now think about this...are you making your life's decisions alone or are you consulting with me? Now, I can see you are worried. Should you say that you are in control of your own life or should you say that you have given your life to me completely? They are both good answers but the best answer is to INCLUDE me in decisions about your life. Don't make them by yourself.

And don't just THROW the decision-making to me. You have free will on earth. You can choose to receive my messages or you can choose your own thoughts. I respect you when you choose your thoughts without my guidance. I know you believe you are capable of handling life in a mature fashion but believe me, there are times when life throws you a zinger and that is where I come in. It is easy to bring me into your life. Just say…'help me, please' and my angels and I will be at your side immediately.

So, again, I ask you…who is the decision maker in your life? I know you WANT it to be you but think about making your decisions WITH me. Always know that I will never demand that you follow my advice because I respect your gift of 'free will'.

Let's work together to develop your soul so that you may have a meaningful experience on earth.

-Jesus

RECEIVE ME

I walk with you and I talk to you.

I am truly with you so why don't you receive me into your life? I know you would be very happy to have me as a part of your life especially when you are troubled.

Look for me. I am the helping hand that picks up your dropped parcel. I am the smile you receive when you are sad. I am the quote that you read that answers your troubling questions in life.

Yes, I see you and hear you and reach out to give you help but you don't recognize me. You believe that the hello from the person you passed on the street was just from a cheery guy. But I saw you passing this 'cheery guy' and inspired him to say hello to you because I knew you were sad.

Seeing me is receiving me and receiving me is opening your heart to me. For without me, life is empty and lonely. You can feel my presence in your heart. Listen to your heart. Listen to what it is telling you.

When you receive advice and comments from others, don't discard them…receive them, think about them, and then turn inward and look into your heart. What is your heart saying? When you receive me, you will hear my messages.

Can you hear me? Do you WANT to hear me?

I have said many times now…the secret to living your life with me is receiving me into your life and listening to your heart. Listen to my messages. They are there. They are big and they are small. They are strong and they are light but they are full of love. Be quiet and listen.

It is your choice.

I am always here and I am always with you.

Receive me.

-Jesus

RECONNECTING

$\mathcal{I}$'ve been waiting to hear from you but there is only silence.

I am trying very hard but I hear nothing from you. Why haven't I heard from you?

I can help you but you must open your heart to me.

Why are you waiting? Why is it taking you so long?

Again, I can see how busy you are. But what is really wrong?

You say, very quietly, that everything is driving you crazy. You whisper that you have no time for yourself. You don't know who you are anymore because your life is so hectic. Yes, I hear you say that you do love your family and your life but you have lost contact with yourself.

Well…you have lost contact with me also.

Reach out to me for I am your way back. Don't be hesitant because you haven't talked to me for a little while. Know that I have been with you constantly. As you search to reconnect with yourself, relax your mind to receive me. When you allow my angels and me into your life you will open the path of connecting with yourself.

You say that you have no idea how to go about 'finding' yourself. You know that you have lost the 'real' you but maybe later would be a good time to reconnect with your true self. Please don't wait until later in your life to find the 'real' you. It is necessary to find yourself now because many of your life's decisions influence you not only today but also in years to come. Don't wait and don't be quietly unhappy because you have lost touch with yourself.

My angels and I are right beside you now and we are waiting for you to ask us into your life. As you receive us, we will show you how to reconnect with yourself and with your soul. You must receive us into your heart for the process to begin.

I see you are interested in finding yourself but you are hesitant. You say that you have no time anymore for yourself let alone any time to give to my angels and me. Our plan would probably work, you say, but not at this time. And I say, there is no better time than now because this is when you need our help the most. You need to reconnect with yourself now.

Start the process of connecting with my angels and with me by thinking of us in the morning and evening and then whisper 'thank you' and 'welcome'. That is all you have to do. We will do the rest. As you relax, visualize a new you standing before you. This is the real you that you have lost contact with. Close your eyes and feel your heart, feel contentment and happiness. Stay there for a moment because you are reconnecting with me.

You may not recognize yourself now. But that is okay because the new 'you' inside is bursting to come out. Release your new persona for the world to see and enjoy. It is the new you who has merged with me.

Take notice of the changes in your life. Life will suddenly look very different to you. It will be friendly, welcoming and less chaotic. Enjoy this newfound peace.

We have now merged and together we are one.

I am part of your life. I AM your life.

Thank you for reconnecting with your soul and receiving me back into your life.

-Jesus

FEAR

I know there is a lot of noise down there on earth, and many times even when I speak loudly no one seems to hear me.

The noise that I hear seems to come from fear. Fear appears to be generated from oppression, starvation, war, poor living conditions, and general malaise. These are legitimate concerns but I also see fear in every day life.

Fear is an all-encompassing feeling. It is a powerful feeling that can engulf and cripple you. But why do you fear? You fear because you are more involved with your human life than your spiritual life. If you remember, you were taught as a child to talk to God during good times as well as fearful times.

I am here for you so why don't you talk to me about your fears? Why don't you ask for my help? I see you complaining many times to your neighbor, to a friend, or a relative, giving them all the details of your life's difficulties and how fear has crept into your life from these difficulties. But you never complain to me!

I can help you more than your neighbors, friends or relatives. Come to me and tell me all that is bothering you. Tell me what you like on earth and tell me what you don't like. Tell me what you fear and tell me what you don't fear.

You do call me for help once in a while when you are totally frustrated. I have heard you scream…'okay, Jesus, what is going on in my life; I don't deserve this' or 'Jesus, how did you let this happen to me; I didn't do anything to you'. Yes, I get these messages and many more like them from many people on earth. I don't mind because I know that in times of total frustration and fear, I am called upon.

If only I were called upon earlier and more often. If only I were always a part of your everyday life. If only…if only…

You may start to incorporate me into your life after reading an article about how an injured person was miraculously healed, or a small child was rescued from a disastrous car crash, or an elderly person escaped death from a house fire with help possibly from an angel. Yes, these articles made you think about your mortality. It seems mortality and the fears of mortality make humans more attentive to the immortality of the soul. However, as time passes, all return to their old routines and forget about me.

Do you NEED me only when disaster strikes? Do you NEED me only when fear is becoming a part of your everyday life? Yes, you need me then as well as everyday when you have no fears. Living with me everyday prepares and protects you from fears that enter your life. It is important to evaluate your fears and determine how much trust you have in me to bring me into your life.

It is easy to remove the fears in your life. You just need to whisper my name daily to make me a part of your life. As I become stronger with you, your fears will automatically be given to me to handle. I will show you how to evaluate each fear as it comes to you. I will teach you how to stand up to each fear and move it out of your life. I will show you the happiness that exists when fear is removed.

Come to me now and give me your fears. Take your time because I know how fearful you are right now but, please, trust me.

Remember, happiness is waiting for you.

I am your happiness.

-Jesus

INDIFFERENCE

I talked about indifference many times during my life on earth but you probably have not heard much about indifference in your lifetime.

Indifference.

Exactly what does this mean to you? It means 'not caring' to me.

It means that if a particular situation in life doesn't relate to you, you pay no attention to it. You basically 'don't care' because you are not directly affected.

But think about it now with me.

You see an article that is heartbreaking about a family in a foreign country who has lost everything due to a massive storm, earthquake, or war. You read the article and you feel a little empathy but you shrug your shoulders and say that is too bad. An organization, named in the article, is asking for your help. Again, you shrug your shoulders. Now, help includes prayers to me, to God, and to the angels, especially, if you are unable to help with their physical needs or help them financially. So you see, just because you cannot help physically or financially does not mean you cannot help. Don't be indifferent to this plea for help. Your prayers and the prayers of those you recruit for this effort ARE significant.

Indifference also occurs in many other areas of life such as politics, troubled neighborhoods, cities and even countries. Again, send them my love, and send them my angels. Surround them with our love. But don't do this once or twice and feel you have done your part in aiding others. Send them this 'spiritual support group' every day.

Don't be indifferent...be involved spiritually.

I know this is strong but I want to convey the message of these words. Mankind has always preferred to look the other way with regard to human suffering. However, human suffering is part of life.

No matter how well you live your life or how upstanding you believe you are or how you believe you are above tragedy...you are not. You are not above anything on earth because that is how it is on the earth plane. Souls incarnate to experience difficulties and souls incarnate to help others.

All are on earth for the purpose of soul development.

So, I say to you...do you want to be indifferent or do you want to be a part of the universal plan to help advance your soul closer to God?

It is your choice.

Remember, I am always here for you. It is up to YOU to choose me to help you and to help the world.

Don't be indifferent.

-Jesus

BELIEFS

$\mathcal{I}$t is the nature of humans to value their earthly possessions especially when they worked their entire lifetime to acquire a level of acceptance as viewed from their possessions.

And I say to you…that's okay. You cannot spend your entire life feeling guilty with what you have worked so hard to earn. In fact, I commend you. I see that you worked hard, you saved, and you rewarded yourself as best you could. Do NOT feel guilty. .

But possessions do not always mean material goods and success. Possessions can also describe your ideals, principals and beliefs.

Your ideals are what you live by. They come from your family and become a part of you as a young child. The principals you possess come from your experiences as a child and as a young adult. The beliefs you hold as an adult are a culmination of the ideals and principals you acquired as a child and young adult. Beliefs are possessions. They are intangible possessions that guide you through life every day. It is your beliefs as an adult that I now want you to evaluate with me.

I hear some resistance right now. You are saying…your beliefs are your beliefs. They are a part of you and you don't want to give them up. I am not asking you to 'give them up'. I am asking you to look very closely at your beliefs and thoroughly scrutinize them.

Now, look into your heart and identify your beliefs. What are your feelings about world events, world tragedies, and world apathy? What do you think about your community, your family structure, and your social structure? Are your spiritual beliefs tainted? Are they full of prejudices that you carried with you as you traveled through life? Do you see the possibility of hate existing within your beliefs? Do you feel these tainted beliefs truly describe you?

Beliefs replete with prejudice, hate, and jealousy will destroy you. They will destroy your physical body and they will destroy your soul.

Remember, you are on earth to advance your soul. Look at yourself and look at your beliefs. Look at them very carefully. Analyze your beliefs: one by one. Now take each belief after you have analyzed it and decide: do I keep it or do I discard it? If you decide to discard it, make sure you truly discard it. Move it completely out of your life forever.

This process may take you several months or several years. And that is okay because you are making a conscious effort to remove unwanted spiritual beliefs from your life. It is like your wardrobe. Many have difficulty discarding even an old, worn sweater because it has been with them for so long that it is virtually a part of their life even though they no longer use it.

So, come to me and give me your unwanted spiritual beliefs. Give me the beliefs that are holding you back from developing your soul.

It is easy but YOU must make the first move.

Do it. Do it for yourself. Do it for me.

-Jesus

THANKFULNESS

*T*here are so many wonderful things to be thankful for on earth.

There is the beautiful earth, which changes her wardrobe every season. Her fall wardrobe is brilliant with color, her winter wardrobe is soft and white with icicles hanging from her trees, her spring wardrobe jumps alive with multicolored flowers and blossoming trees, and her summer wardrobe is warm and full of energy from the sun.

Yes, a touch of beauty surrounds everyone on earth. Some people enjoy it and even look forward to the beauty of each season. Many send a special 'thank you' to me each season for this beauty.

But for those who are not tuned into nature, there are many other reasons to live a happy and thankful life.

Look at your life now. Look at the good side.

I already hear you moaning. You say you do not have a good side in your life. And I say…yes you do. Everyone has a good and happy side no matter how many difficulties you may be experiencing.

Look at your life closely now and analyze it. With all your moaning and groaning while looking ONLY at your difficulties did you remember to look into your heart? Or have you also abandoned your heart, which is your message center from God?

This message center, your heart, will reveal to you why you are presently experiencing difficulties. Your heart will tell you how to accept your current situation and how to move through difficult times. Your heart may even guide you to another who has far more difficulties in life than you, but there is always a smile on that person's face. Stop when you see this. Go and find out how that person can be truly happy when their life appears so shattered. Know that I directed you to that person.

Don't abandon any opportunity to change your life. Once you see and understand and accept all of life's experiences as growing steps for your soul, you will be thanking me every day and twice on Sunday, as the saying goes. For without these life experiences, your soul is stagnant. It is not growing. It is becoming dull and losing its light that shines for God.

So I want you to look at your life again. As you progress, your heart will feel lighter and smiles will come easier to you. Thank everyone who comes your way…even the stranger who passes you on the street and offers you a smile and a nod that says 'hello'.

Being thankful is a feeling that comes from the heart. Open your heart to receive my love and pass it on by being thankful.

Be thankful for your family and friends. Be thankful for your life and what you are learning from it. Be thankful for your environment and what it is teaching you, and be thankful for the true beauty of the earth that surrounds you.

Whisper 'thank you' as you see the beauty of the trees, the meadows, the sky, the sea, the mountains and the desert. When I hear your thankfulness, I will know you are truly moving your life towards love and happiness.

You are moving your life towards me.

-Jesus

VIOLENCE

*T*he earth has always been an environment where humans like to air their differences with each other in some sort of combative way. It may be verbal, physical or even mental. Know that it is okay to spar with each other if there is no harm intended.

But, there has been a significant increase in intentional physical harm to innocent bystanders. Why is this occurring? Why do humans want to cause injury to each other? Life on earth is extremely difficult. Why add another layer of difficulty with arguments, with hatred and with guns? This really saddens me.

Destroying and conquering are not the answers. History has proven that violence has never been the answer for world peace.

I hear you saying that there have been times when evil and destructive humans needed to be stopped as they forged a bloody trail to conquer and rule the existing world. And I say, yes, that is true. But once the destructive humans have been contained, the rest of the world must look to each other to unite to build a new world of love.

But, human competitiveness continues to exist and with it the desire to conquer and rule. This need to rule has crept into the minds and hearts of the very young. I see societies teaching their children and young adults about weaponry. I also see young people turning to violence for excitement without realizing the consequences of injury or killing. This saddens me tremendously. What is happening on earth that is causing violence to be needed and accepted?

Has the earth forgotten me? My life ended in violence but that does not mean violence should be accepted and continued. My life on earth is not to be remembered on a violent note. It is to be remembered for the love that I taught. Violence only begets violence.

You read of violence in the newspapers. You hear about violence on television. You see violence on Facebook. However, no one ever calls my name to help the injured, or to help the perpetrators, or to help society. Your cities, towns, states and countries must begin to heal. All have been badly damaged by the pervasive hate that exists on earth.

Call on me and call on my angels. Every time you hear or see a destructive or violent act, call me. Ask me to come to the violence to calm it. Ask me to come to the injured to heal them. Ask me to come to those who are committing the crime and ask me to intercede. Ask me to show them the destruction they are causing, the hatred that is in their hearts and why it is there. Ask me to help them to see their darkened hearts.

You must raise awareness. You must raise the minds of all who are working for peace by asking me to guide and protect them. You must raise the minds of those who are being influenced to follow a destructive way of life by asking me to intercede and to help stop their negative behavior.

Call on my angels and call on me.

Violence is NOT a part of God. And the sooner the human race realizes this…the sooner peace will come to humankind. That alone sounds like a miracle, doesn't it? Well, it IS a miracle and it CAN happen. Be a part of this miracle.

Start today. Start a chain of prayers on Facebook or other social media to stop violence on earth. There WILL be peace on earth…be a part of this peace process.

Remember…violence begets violence and peace begets peace.

You were born with God and God is peace so you are peace.

Return to this peace. Return to love.

Return to God.

-Jesus

VISITATION

*V*isitation. What is your first thought when you hear this word?

You may picture visiting with your family, or visiting someone in the hospital, or visiting those who are alone in your community, or just visiting your friends for fun.

Yes, the word conjures thoughts of helping, good will, and smiles.

But, have you ever thought of 'visiting' with me?

Every weekend you visit with your family or your friends to enjoy time together but I never seem to be included in your visits.

With new technology that is available now, you are able to visit and virtually see your friends and family even when you live many miles apart. I know you can't see me physically but if you call me as you call your friends, I will answer. You will feel my love in your heart and if you quiet your mind you will hear my words.

You are moving through life very fast now so please slow up, rest your mind, and rest your body. You are very busy trying to stay 'in touch' with your immediate world. Put down your IPhones and your computers for just one day and come 'visit' with me. Visit me for just one day to receive a relaxing retreat.

And a relaxing retreat it will be and it won't cost you a penny. My advice is free!!! Go to where you will not be disturbed. Go to where you are comfortable. Remove all your fears about disconnecting from your world.

Now, just say my name, and nothing else. I will hear you and I will know you are in a quiet state to receive me. When you start hearing me, please talk to me. Tell me, as you do with your friends and family, how your day is going. Are you frustrated with anything? I hear many frustrating conversations when you are on your IPhone and when you text. Tell them also to me.

I am here to listen AND to help you. I will send you angels and archangels to help you through difficult times. What are you waiting for? All you have to do is learn to quiet your mind, come visit with me and ask me for advice and help. I would like to renew our friendship.

'Visiting' with me daily strengthens your physical being as well as your spiritual being. Your physical being will be strengthened by your ability to release tension and bad feelings.

Spiritually, your soul will grow tremendously. And that is important because you, and everyone around you, are here to grow your soul closer to God. All is quiet for your soul right now and it has been for a little while. Let's wake it up!

I know your soul and I know it would enjoy visiting with me again. So, please don't delay. I am waiting for you to pick up your phone in your mind's eye and call me.

I am waiting. Your soul is waiting. God is waiting.

Do it now. Do it for yourself. Do it for your soul.

-Jesus

MYSTERIOUS

$\mathscr{S}$o, how many of you think that I am mysterious or that I am a secret?

I hear many say 'yes' that you do not understand me and therefore you believe I am a secret that you do not feel the need to figure out.

That is a common belief. However, I am not difficult to understand but you make it difficult because you WANT to make me mysterious.

My angels and I are with you at all times guiding and protecting you while you are on earth. However, many do not recognize my presence and my help and therefore, I am labeled as 'mysterious' or even 'non-existent'.

But let's get back to you. I know you believe in me. You know that I am present for you. Your beliefs are strong so why do you consider me mysterious or secret? What are you afraid of? Are you afraid that I might force you to face reality sometime in your life? Are you afraid that I might force you to look very hard into your heart to see yourself? Are you afraid of seeing the real you?

So you see, it is not I who is mysterious…it is you. It is you hiding from your true self.

I say to you now, call on me. Call me and I will help you to see your true self. I will help you 'like' yourself. You know that it is very important in life to like yourself. How can you like others and be kind to others when you do not like yourself and you are not kind to yourself? Think about that.

Let me help you learn to know and to like yourself. Look for God's peace and beauty that surrounds you, recognize it, and make it a part of you. Opening up and finding yourself, and finding me, will reward you with a level of happiness and inner peace that knows no comparison in your life. You will be smiling, your heart will be dancing, and all the struggles and disappointments that may come your way will be received with openness, strength, and a will to move forward.

So, come, and join me in search of you. For it is you who is mysterious and secret and not I. Come to me and ask for help and guidance for you to see your soul. Remember, to see your soul is to see me and to see me is to see God. I am one with you and one with God. Remove the mystery cloud.

What are you waiting for?

Release your soul to me and enter my world...a world that is open, loving, and free.

I am not hidden. I am not mysterious. I am not secretive.

Please come.

-Jesus

SPIRITUAL REPORT

*H*ow many times per day do I hear these words echoing from the earth plane…'this is your heart report, this is your cholesterol report, this is your diabetes report, or this is your kidney report'?

So what about your spiritual report?

I already hear you exclaiming…exactly WHAT is a 'spiritual report'? Is it necessary for my survival?

You go through many physical tests in life all with the goal of extending your time on earth. But, really, how long do you want to live? The real answer is 'not forever'.

BUT, your soul DOES live forever!!!

You work very hard to keep your body in decent working condition and rightfully so, but there are very few people working to improve their souls. I know you feel it is important to keep your body in good shape as you age but why don't you work as hard to maintain a strong and healthy soul?

How, you might ask, do I maintain a strong and healthy soul? And my answer is…Meditation! Meditation!! Meditation!!! And you say that you don't have any time for meditation. And I say…that just doesn't make sense to me.

Many get out of bed an hour early to exercise but have you ever thought that this is a good time to meditate? Think about it. You ask…how can this be? You thought that a person needed to be still to meditate. You only need to be still within yourself.

Ask the angels or me to join you in your exercise/meditative routine. You will feel our presence as an overwhelming feeling of peace and love in your being. As you continue on with this process, recognize when we are with you and start communicating with us. This is when the soul development process begins.

You now ask how can you meditate when you don't like to exercise? There are many opportunities. Become aware of the times when you are alone and turn your thoughts to my angels and me. It is that simple and the more you practice calling on us during your quiet times the more your meditative process will become a part of you. Once meditation is a regular part of your life, you will recognize my angels and I working with you. Your heart will become attuned to our presence. This is the beginning of soul development. As you grow stronger working with us, your 'spiritual report' will show a significant improvement.

Soul development is so much easier than physical development, but physical development always wins out over spiritual because it is perceived as being more important for living on earth.

Your body is your body and you are already attuned to keeping it in good physical shape.

Your soul is your soul and unless you do something soon, it will become weak and grow away from me. You are my best friend and I will help you monitor and improve your 'spiritual' report.

Friends do that you know…they are always there to help you.

-Jesus

ADVICE

I would like to give one more piece of advice to humankind.

I always receive many requests for help but many of those requests involve survival...survival following the death of a loved one, survival to overcome drug addictions and abuse, survival from paycheck to paycheck. All these requests tell me just how miserable and unhappy many souls are with their lives on earth.

There are no requests from these souls asking for help to UNDERSTAND the difficulties they are presently experiencing. They just say...'why me', or 'this is unfair', or 'I am a good person, why are you punishing me'?

We are not 'punishing you' and we know you feel your suffering is unfair. But, I want you to look very closely at what you are experiencing and look closely at your heart. I hear you exclaim...'my heart'!!! What has that got to do with my cancer, my child's illness, or my inability to care for my family? Technically speaking...nothing. Spiritually speaking... everything.

Where is your heart right now and please don't say it is in the middle of your chest! I am referring to the FEELINGS in your heart. Is your heart sad and lonely? Is it hurt and hardened? Is it angry? Is it jealous? Is it happy but guarded? Do you harbor many of these feelings while giving the impression that everything is okay in your life following a cancer treatment or the loss of a loved one?

This is what I want you to evaluate. Come to me and describe this hurt. For it is by working through this pain with me that you will be able to move closer to God. I can help you with this pain but you MUST come to me. Tell me how you feel and ask me to help you understand your pain.

By understanding the difficulties your heart holds, you can more easily work through the pain and transition to a happy, loving and kind heart that is aligned with God. I am here to help you through this. Together we can make this a step-by-step procedure. First, talk to me about your physical problems. I have heard them before but it is okay to repeat them. Next, tell me exactly how you feel inside and don't hold back. Talk about EVERYTHING that is hurting you.

If tears come to your eyes that is good, for you are showing me that you are truly releasing the feelings that may have been hidden for many years. These feelings can accumulate over time without you being aware that you had tucked them away in a corner of your heart.

So, go ahead, cry. Cry hard because with each tear that is falling, I am removing all the pain in your heart. Once your tears have dried, sit quietly and call me. Your heart is clear now and your pain is gone. Feel me as I enter your heart. Your heart will feel light. It will feel love and it will feel happy. This may be strange to you since it has been a long time since you have truly been with me.

I am here for you. You can be stubborn and believe that you are strong enough to handle anything that life gives you, and maybe you are. However, it is much easier when you invite me into your life and ask me for my advice.

It is your choice because you have free will. You can request my help or you can do it your way. Think about it.

I am just offering you a few words of advice.

As the saying goes: take it or leave it.

I hope you take it because I give you advice out of my love for you.

-Jesus

AS YOU ARE

$\mathscr{I}$ say to you…stay as you are. You are beautiful to me.

I don't see why you worry so much about your appearance. I hear you say that you see how organized and together others appear to be, or how talented or intelligent they are and that you believe that you can never perform as they do. Why do you feel the need to 'measure up'? The others that you observe are just living their own lives.

Why the competition? You are all different individuals on earth working on the development of your own souls. A comment I hear many times is that others are advancing in life faster than you. That is not necessarily so. Your fellow workers or friends or neighbors may be advancing in life because they are in union with their inner selves. Are you? I see that you look puzzled. I see that you don't understand. I know you are extremely competent in all that you do. So, it is now time for you to look inside your heart.

Your heart will tell you when you are making right and wrong decisions, but you must be open to listening to the messages from your heart. Right now, I see you are not ready to listen to your heart. You are focused on the outside and not on the inside, on the human side of your life and not on your soul side.

Now, I ask you, do you want to operate from the inside, your soul, or from the outside, your physical being? Do you want to be who you really are?

Your soul is your true identity. To see your soul, you must go through your heart. Your heart has feelings, and you have learned to turn your 'heart feelings' off. Yet it is through your heart feelings that true communication with your soul occurs. Know that your soul communicates to your heart and your heart communicates to your conscious self.

So, how do I learn to open my heart to hear and know my soul, you ask?

Commit to meditating daily and you will begin to receive a stream of words from me. They will be short in the beginning but as you get stronger in your meditation, my messages will get louder and longer. Keep a journal of my messages. As your heart begins to open and receive my messages, your soul will also open to reveal the real you.

Be aware of the 'real' you. Many will ask you what is happening in your life because you seem so peaceful and happy. And all that you did to make this happen was to open your heart and reacquaint yourself with the real you.

The real you is your soul experiencing a human form on earth. Always remember that. Do not try to be someone else because you cannot. You are as you are.

Call on me, anytime, to help you be as you truly are.

-Jesus

BELIEVE

*W*HO ARE YOU?

Do you know? Do your care?

Have you ever asked yourself this question?

It is interesting but not many people have ever asked this question. Of course there are some...the deep thinkers, the philosophers, the spiritualists. But the majority of people on earth have never even thought about who they really are and why they are here.

I believe many do not care about their spiritual life.

Materialism is prevalent all over the world and is the driving force for a large number of souls on earth. Even the souls who exist in extreme poverty have not looked at themselves and asked the questions...'who am I', and 'why am I here'. This is all very sad to me because I see that these souls believe that they exist just to survive. There is so much more than 'just surviving' life on earth.

You are here to experience good times and bad times. You are here to learn from the good times and to learn from the bad times. You are here to advance your soul with the good times as well as the bad times. Enjoy the good times and look at the bad times, the difficult times, as learning blocks.

I know many of you are now saying to yourself...'how can cancer be a learning block, or how can a tragic car accident be a learning block, or how can autism or Alzheimer's be learning blocks'? They are very difficult learning blocks, I agree, but you must look at them as soul development steps to advance your soul.

And exactly what is soul development, I hear you asking.

Soul development is the process by which a soul CHOOSES to advance its soul toward perfection in the eyes of God. However, a soul must first learn to know, to recognize and to believe in itself. Once it has accomplished that, it can move on to receive and learn from earth's experiences.

Now, look at your life, as it is today. What are you experiencing on the human level? Is it sickness? Is it loneliness? Is it despair? Is it deep-seated anger? Whatever you see in your life, look at it long and hard and accept that the feeling is a part of you.

I want you to come to me because I want to explain to you why you are experiencing life as you are. I want to show you what is needed in your life in order to grow your soul.

Remember, you are not suffering on earth for nothing. When you receive these challenges, acknowledge the difficulty involved. By accepting the difficulty, you will then be moving your soul to a higher level with God. I am not saying that it is an easy process but if you start to open your mind and your heart to your challenges, you will be able to accept them more easily.

So, please, believe in yourself as I believe in you.

You are a child of God and you are of God. Never, ever think or believe that God has abandoned you. It doesn't work that way.

I am here waiting for you to call. Just say my name and welcome me into your heart. I will walk with you through life. I will show you how to grow your soul and enjoy your time on earth.

Believe in me as I believe in you.

-Jesus

Printed in the United States
By Bookmasters